An Aviation Adventure

A History of Aviation in Nashville, Tennessee and
The Metropolitan Nashville Airport Authority

Printed in the United States of America
First Printing 2003

Metropolitan Nashville Airport Authority
One Terminal Drive, Nashville, TN 37214-4114

Library of Congress Catalog Card Number: 2003115030
ISBN 1-59512-000-9

 *This book is dedicated to the late John Childress Tune, in recognition of and appreciation for his many years of leadership in aviation, his determination and wise guidance in forming the Metropolitan Nashville Airport Authority and his commitment to making the dream take wing.*

Introduction
by
Raul L. Regalado, C.A.E.
President and CEO
Metropolitan Nashville Airport Authority

The Nashville Airport is operated by an Airport Authority, which is the organizational structure that makes the most sense for managing a major city's aviation facilities and service.

The Nashville Airport over the years has enjoyed tremendous support from business and civic leadership, and a broad base of Nashvillians. That support is documented frequently in the pages that follow.

And then there is the appeal of the city itself, which offers a high quality of life, based on strong family values. In other words, it's just a fine place to live.

I have been associated with a number of airports that have no written history and incomplete records of how they came about and grew.

I salute the members of the Airport Authority for commissioning this written record of aviation in Nashville, while there are those who can provide an historic and institutional knowledge of the facts and preserve them for future generations.

And I look forward to, with you, being a personal part of future chapters to be written about this exciting part of our city and its growth.

Background

On Dec.17, 1903, two brothers from Dayton, Ohio, went into the history books with the first successful powered, controlled, heavier-than-air machine flight. Crawling to a prone position between the wings of a biplane he and his bother Wilbur had built, Orville Wright opened the throttle of a homemade 12 horsepower machine and lifted off the sand dunes at Kitty Hawk, North Carolina. The first flight lasted but 12 seconds and covered a mere 120 feet, but by day's end, they had made four flights. In one of those four, Wilbur was airborne 59 seconds and traveled 852 feet.

This great adventure we know as aviation may have started with the Wright brothers that day on North Carolina's Outer Banks, but it wasn't limited to the area around Kitty Hawk, North Carolina.

The City of Nashville, Tennessee, has shared in and contributed to the growth of commercial aviation in this country and the world.

From its humble beginnings, marked by the first flights into and out of this area in the early 1900s, through the dawn of national commercial aviation and continuing today, Nashville and Middle Tennessee have played a prominent role in aviation's great adventure. Along the way, this region has created "one of the five best airports in the world," * thanks to the vision of several community-minded citizens and a concept of governance best described with one simple word: "genius."

---

* Captain Eddie Rickenbacker, WWI flying ace and V.P. and general manager, Eastern Air Lines, made this declaration at the official dedication of Nashville Municipal Airport on Nov. 1, 1936.

Contents

Introduction v
Background vi
Chapter 1 – The Beginning of the Adventure 1
Chapter 2 – Nashville Embraces Aviation 9
Chapter 3 – The War Years – Military Management 25
Chapter 4 – Post World War II: City Government 29
Chapter 5 – A New Age for Aviation Dawns in Middle Tennessee 41
Chapter 6 – Operating in a Regulated Environment 57
Chapter 7 – New Leadership and Growth Under Deregulation 65
Chapter 8 – Overcoming the Obstacles 77
Chapter 9 – A New Airport Terminal and Runway for Nashville 85
Chapter 10 – Diversified Services in a Deregulated Economy 93
Chapter 11 – Reaping the Benefits of Quality Air Service 103
Chapter 12 – The Future of Aviation in Nashville 113
Chapter 13 – Giving Credit Where Credit is Due 121
Chapter 14 – The MNAA – A Model Airport Authority 131
Chapter 15 – A Time of Transition 141
Appendixes
   Appendix A – MNAA Board of Commissioners 145
   Appendix B – Bibliography/Sources 146
   Appendix C – Acknowledgements/Credits 151

The Beginning of the Adventure

Chapter 1

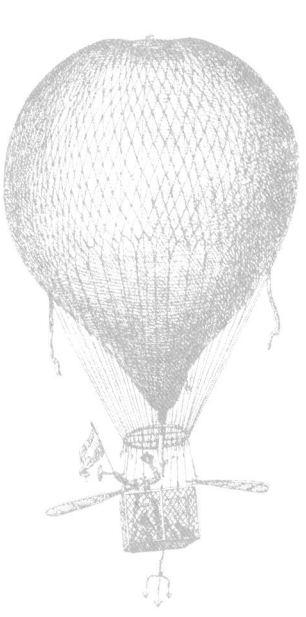

Chapter 1
The Beginning of the Adventure

The first recorded flight in the Nashville area was in 1842 when balloon flight came to Tennessee and Nashville. In his book Aviation in Tennessee, author Jim Fulbright reports that one of Nashville's earliest exhibitions involved balloon pioneer Richard Clayton. On March 30, 1842, Clayton sold tickets ($1 for adults and 50 cents for children) to those who wanted to witness this balloon exhibition as he lifted off from downtown to float some 17 miles east-southeast of Nashville.

The turnout was small that day. Perhaps, citizens were more concerned with making Nashville the permanent capital of the state, which happened the following year in 1843.

In the ensuing years, Nashville flourished. Steamboats lined the city's wharf and rail service came to Nashville. Thanks to the city's strategic location on the river and as a rail center, prosperity continued until 1860. Nashville's central location brought occupation by federal troops for three years during the Civil War. The last aggressive action of the Confederate Army came in 1864 when the Battle of Nashville was fought, and won handily by Union forces.

Devastated by the Civil War, Nashville began the process of rebuilding. Then, as today, aviation played a role in that rebirth. Just a dozen years after the War Between the States ended, Nashville's aviation adventure took flight with an historic hot air balloon launch.

On June 17, 1877, Nashville established its pioneering position in the history of airmail. On that day, a hot air balloon, the Buffalo, piloted by Samuel Archer King, ascended in Nashville carrying what was then reported as the first mail ever to go by aircraft. This bit of history was unearthed by some stamp collectors' research and reported in an article in the Aug. 25, 1935, edition of the Nashville Banner. Calling June 17 a "red-letter day for Nashville," the article also reported the ascent drew thousands of spectators who came by foot, buggy, wagon and train.

No one knew when the Buffalo lifted off that day in 1877 from the corner of Broadway and Spence Street (now 8th Avenue) and floated 26 miles to Gallatin that this was the forerunner of an important worldwide postal system. The letters carried by the Buffalo for the first time bore an adhesive postage stamp printed specifically for airmail.

Soon inventors progressed from balloons to flying machines.

Nashville had its share of early "dreamers" who experimented with flight. Professor Arthur Barnard built his Centennial airship "in a barn-like building on the grounds of what is now Centennial Park," author Jim Fulbright wrote. On May 6, 1897, this YMCA instructor flew his airship 20 miles west of Nashville and, when the evening winds changed, was able to return to the city.

Professor Barnard's flight in Nashville came six years before Orville and Wilbur Wright's historic flight at Kitty Hawk in 1903.

World Wars I and II Spark Growth of Aviation

Nashville, at the turn of the century, had a population of 80,865 and by 1910, this number had risen to more than 110,000, making it among the largest and fastest growing cities in the South. Electric streetcars and newfangled automobiles filled the streets. The railway system now complimented the river as a transportation and distribution center and helped Nashville become a regional trade and manufacturing center. The area was enjoying the prosperity of the pre-war era.

Nashville registered another mark in the annals of aviation history on June 22, 1910. Charles K. Hamilton, reportedly the "premier stunt pilot" of the day, while participating in a Grand Military Tournament at Nashville's fairgrounds, made aviation's first night flight. He first took off at 7:30 p.m., CST, and simply flew around the fairgrounds. A bit more daring, he attached a spotlight to his aircraft and took off again at 10:57 p.m., and enthralled the crowds below who watched this tiny "speck of light" sail through the air. This flight lasted 18 minutes before Hamilton had to glide back to earth when the cylinder head on his engine blew out. For his efforts, tournament officials gave him a medal for performing "the first nocturnal flight ever made by an aviator driving an airplane."

Four years later on Nov. 17, 1914, aviatrix Katherine Stinson, only the fourth American woman to hold a pilot's license from the Federation Aeronautique Internationale, gave an aerial exhibition in Nashville (later in 1939, her family would build the Stinson aircraft plant next to Nashville's Berry Field).

The beginning of World War I in Europe in 1914 escalated the need for aircraft. Only a few planes were being manufactured per year in Europe at the time. In 1914, the U.S. Army Signal Corps ordered what is believed to be the world's finest military plane. The government paid $30,000 for a specially built Wright Plane. When the U.S. entered the war in 1917, the country had only about 110 military planes. By war's end in 1918, the U.S. had built almost 15,000 military planes.

The Mail Takes to the Air

These military planes soon were put to good use. Army planes flew the mail between New York City, Philadelphia and Washington, D.C., when the U.S. Government inaugurated the world's first permanent airmail service on May 15, 1918. Soon Army planes carried mail regularly for the Post Office Department, making one round trip a day (except Sunday) between the nation's capital and New York City. On Aug. 12, 1918, the Post Office also began contracting with private airlines to carry the mail.

Nashville's importance in the history of airmail was enhanced in 1924 when it became the first city in the South from which mail was flown to the North by airplane.

On July 29, 1924, two Army pilots took off from Blackwood Field (one of Nashville's first airstrips), carrying a pouch of mail bound for Chicago. According to the Nashville Banner (June 13, 1937), Capt. Herbert Fox and Lt. V. J. Meloy took off in an Army "Flaming Coffin," a DH-4BM-1. Fox was with the 105th Observation Squadron and the foreign and exchange teller for American National Bank. (He would later become the state's director of aeronautics.) Meloy was in the regular Army air service and instructor for the Squadron.

Approval for the flight and instructions for handling the first class mail had come by telegram the day before from the Post Office Department in Washington, D.C.

Dr. W. J. Callahan, then Nashville postmaster, had sworn in the city's first "air mailmen" and gave the two pilots pistols to protect "Uncle Sam's precious cargo" – a mail pouch containing 150 pounds of banking items worth $226,128.73.

Visitors held up lanterns for the pre-dawn take off at 4 a.m. The pilots were literally flying blind with no modern day instruments to guide them as they headed their plane north and flew at an average speed of 120 mph until daylight came. Using recognizable landmarks below, they made it to Chicago and landed at Maywood Field three hours and 29 minutes later. Chicago's mayor and other dignitaries treated them as guests of honor at breakfast.

Although this was termed a "wild success," the first airmail event didn't bring the establishment of regular airmail service to Nashville. That would come four years later, after the Kelly Air Mail Act of 1925 gave private airlines the job of flying mail. Contract Air Mail (C.A.M.) routes, each with a special number, were developed in late 1925 and soon blanketed the country. (These C.A.M. routes eventually would develop into the nation's domestic airline system.)

While the airmail service was in its infancy, Nashville was among the first Southern cities to be served. Interstate Airlines pioneered C.A.M 30 through Nashville, and regular airmail service was inaugurated here Nov. 19, 1928. (Interstate Airlines, Inc., was owned by a holding company known as Aviation Corporation. A pioneer of scheduled commercial aviation in Nashville, this airline would become American Airways by 1930 and later American Airlines.)

Passengers Get on Board Along with the Mail

The first airmail and passenger service in Nashville involved two airplanes flying to and from the city on Dec.1, 1928. According to the Tennessean (Dec. 2, 1928), the "Miss Chattanooga" was the first airmail and passenger plane ever to leave Nashville. This big Fairchild FC-2W plane, which originated in Chattanooga, lifted off from McConnell Field at 12:45 p.m. on Dec. 1, 1928, with Jordan Myers as pilot. Miss Evelyn Norton with Joy's Floral Company of Nashville and W.B. Howland, the city editor of the evening Tennessean, were passengers.

The plane made stops in Evansville and Terre Haute, Ind., and Champaign, Ill. In Champaign, the plane's wheels sank down in the soft soil at the north end of the field. Howland and two other passengers picked up in Terre Haute, had to get out and push the right wing as the pilot gunned the engine to free the plane for take off. "Miss Chattanooga" and her four passengers plus 17 sacks of mail, soared over Chicago shortly after 5 p.m. Guided by a huge search light, the plane landed at Chicago's Municipal Airport at 5:20 p.m.

Army pilots and the Post Office Department had pioneered the early airmail routes. The 1920s saw these routes extended from New York City to San Francisco and the formation of small passenger airlines. They lasted only a few months because of lack of customers. The general public still considered flying a dangerous sport instead of a safe and viable means of transportation.

By the 1930s, however, private companies were handling the flying. As airmail and air cargo service blossomed, so did airline passenger service.

Aviation Continues to Make Giant Leaps

While the general public was hesitant to take to the air, military pilots were quick to embrace this "dangerous sport." Aviation history had been made May 2-3, 1923, when Lts. John A. Macready and Oakley Kelly flew nonstop from New York to San Diego. Their single-engine Fokker T-2 covered the more than 2,500 miles in 26 hours and 50 minutes.

As early as 1919, military pilots had teamed up to make hops across the Atlantic. They had even flown around the world in 1924 when four U.S. Army Air Corps pilots took off from Seattle on April 6. Two of those planes, piloted by Lt. Lowell Smith and Lt. Erik Nelson, landed back in Seattle 175 days and some 26,000 plus miles later. However, it wasn't until 1927 that aviation found another hero to immortalize. Charles Augustus Lindbergh flew his Spirit of St. Louis, a Wright-powered Ryan monoplane, from Roosevelt Field on Long Island, New York, to Le Bourget Field just outside Paris, France, on May 20-21 that year. This first solo transatlantic flight covered 3,610 miles, took 33 hours and 29 minutes to complete and stimulated interest in aviation in the U.S.

Airplanes had become important means of transportation by the time the 1930s rolled around. When the Air Commerce Act, the first federal law to regulate aviation in the U.S., was passed in 1926, airlines were carrying only about 6,000 passengers. In 1930, this number had jumped to more than 400,000. In 1935, the U.S. had five major domestic airlines – American, Eastern, Transcontinental and Western Air (later called Trans World Airlines) and United. Braniff, Delta and Northwest were then smaller regional airlines. Pan American World Airways (Pan Am) was the only major international airline.

In 1938, the year the Civil Aeronautics Authority was established, the world's airlines carried nearly three and one-half million passengers. Flying truly had become an important means of travel. Flying took on an even larger role as the world saw the beginning of another major war in 1939. The military once again greatly influenced aviation's growth.

By the end of World War II in 1945, U.S. factories had churned out more than 300,000 aircraft.

Enter the Jet Age

The end of the war also signaled the beginning of the jet age. Although British inventor Frank Whittle had built the first successful jet engine in 1937, aircraft manufacturers didn't begin developing jet airliners until after World War II. British Overseas Airways Corporation started jet passenger service as early as 1952 but didn't cross the Atlantic until 1958.

(Interestingly enough, on Sept. 22, 1987, Nashville welcomed the arrival of the British Airways Concorde to Nashville's airport, located some 10 miles from the Cumberland River which brought its first settlers to this area just 207 years earlier. The famed SST picked up passengers for a chartered flight to London.)

Deregulation Removes Economic Controls

The new technology in aircraft wasn't the only factor influencing aviation in the 1970s. The Airline Deregulation Act passed by the U.S. Congress in 1978 provided the gradual removal of operating and economic controls over the airline industry. The Civil Aeronautics Board believed that easing controls over airline fares and routes in this country would encourage greater competition and better service. With deregulation came rapid expansion of services through the hub and spoke system created by existing major air carriers and, initially, the formation of new airlines.

Coupled with these changes was an increase in general aviation as airplanes were used for pleasure flying, land surveying, farming and providing an alternative form of travel for business flyers. Increasingly, airplanes were used for hauling cargo. In the U.S. alone, cargo traffic had grown from 0 ton-miles (one ton carried one mile) to 20,510 millions of ton-miles in 1997. Worldwide, since 1945 when accurate totals data became available, cargo traffic had grown to 72,480 millions of ton-miles (one ton equals 2,000 pounds).

In the 1960s, about 100 million passengers were flying on the world's airlines. Today about one and one-half billion people fly annually on these airlines.

Nashville International Airport served 8.0 million of these passengers in 2002 and processed 62.5 thousand tons of cargo during that same period. Truly, Nashville had become part of this international boom in aviation. This was not always the case. Nashville's aviation adventure actually began in a small pasture in what is now a quiet residential neighborhood in the Green Hills area of the city.

Tennessee's Sky Harbor — "NASHVILLE'S AIR MAIL STOP" on a busy d[ay]

Nashville Embraces Aviation

Chapter 2

Chapter 2
Nashville Embraces Aviation

Only eight years passed from the time the Wright brothers made their first public flight in 1908 until Nashville had its first designated airfield. In 1916, E. L. Hampton's pasture became Hampton Field when transfer airplanes began landing there during World War I. The 2,000 foot-long runway's north boundary was along Woodmont Boulevard.

Hampton Field remained Nashville's first airfield for about five years until Blackwood Field opened in 1921. Considered Nashville's first municipal airfield, Blackwood Field, located along Shute Lane and Lebanon Road in Hermitage, was used until 1928.

Blackwood Field was the site for several important milestones in Nashville's aviation history, including the historic first airmail flight in 1924. That same year, the Nashville Aeronautic Corporation (NAC) became Nashville's first commercial air enterprise. NAC owned two planes and operated out of a corner of Blackwood Field. The company offered sightseeing rides, aerial photography and flight instruction. Walter M. Williams, who would later become commander of the 105th Squadron, headed up this firm. One of his first students was Louis Gasser. Gasser in the 1930s would own and operate his own commercial aviation venture, Nashville Flying Service, at McConnell Field.

The City Constructs its First Airfield

McConnell Field was created because Nashville needed a new airfield to keep up with the growth in aviation. The city's first constructed airport opened in 1924 off Murphy Road. Named in memory of Lt. Brower McConnell, a Nashville native and member of the 105th Observation Squadron, McConnell Field lay southwest of 46th and Colorado Avenues expanding west to Richland Creek and south to the railroad. The site for the 131-acre field dated back to 1918, according to George Boyles' article "I Remember Nashville" in the Nashville Scene (1989).

Boyles claims the first airfield began in early summer of 1918 when a small biplane developed operational problems and came down on a vacant lot on Idaho Avenue just west of 46th. Local politician and businessman Warren Sloan, "with a shrewd eye for profit," realized flying's possibilities and turned his worn out cornfield into a valuable asset. "After a couple of years of careful string pulling," Boyles wrote, Sloan would sell the field to the city for its first municipal airfield – McConnell Field.

An early photo of Nashville, taken by Lt W.E. Barr from a plane flown by Capt. Herbert Fox, showed the growing importance of aviation for the city. To guide transient fliers, the first rooftop marker in Nashville appeared on the top of the American Trust Company. This "sky sign" in 10-foot letters read: "Nashville 3M to Field" and included a long arrow pointing west, thus guiding aviators to McConnell Field, the new municipal airport.

Flying was a new "sport" for some. Reportedly, pilots sitting around McConnell Field who needed to know what time it was simply hopped into a plane and flew around Vanderbilt's clock tower and back to the field and reported the time.

The growth of Blackwood and McConnell Fields was due in large part to the Tennessee Air National Guard and the U.S. Mail Service.

Military's Influence Began Prior to World War II

"Nashville's commercial aviation was born in a military airplane and military pilots were the midwives," began a newspaper article, which also recounted the first airmail flight out of Blackwood Field in 1924 by two pilot members of the 105th Observation Squadron. During the 1920s, military aircraft flew out of Blackwood and then McConnell Fields in Nashville. In fact, the primary purpose of the fields was to serve the 105th Observation Squadron.

Tennessee's unit was an outgrowth of the 105th Aero Squadron organized at Kelly Field in San Antonio, Texas, on Aug. 27, 1917. After World War I, during the latter part of 1919, all rated pilots residing in the Nashville area gathered to organize an air unit to function as part of the National Guard in Tennessee. After the National Defense Act of 1920 passed on June 4 of that year, there was a mad rush to become the first air unit in Tennessee. Fierce competition raged between Nashville and Memphis because the state could have only one squadron. And the lucky winner would get a wireless telegraphing station as part of the squadron's work.

On Jan. 1, 1921, the U.S. Militia Bureau sent a telegram to Adjutant General Sweeney informing him that the Tennessee Aviation Unit would be accepted and receive federal recognition after a federal officer inspected it and it met all requirements regarding personnel, operating facilities, flying field, etc.

On May 17, 1921, W.H. Lambeth, chairman of the landing field committee of the Commercial Club of Nashville, a forerunner of the Chamber of Commerce, reported that an aero squadron had been organized as part of the Tennessee National Guard. The state had rented a flying field for six years for $1,500 per year. At the time, he noted, there were no funds to equip the field with necessary hangars and repair shops. The squadron had appealed to the Club for $4,000 in assistance.

A month later on June 9, the secretary of the Commercial Club reported that a fund-raising campaign had raised $3,000 of the amount needed, and Nashville businessman H.O. Blackwood had underwritten the remaining $1,000. The state's adjutant general named the landing field Blackwood Field because of his liberal donation.

Federal recognition for the unit came on Dec. 4, 1921. The squadron flew four new Curtiss JN-6HG "Jennys" and one DH-4B DeHavilland aircraft. By 1924, it was flying Martin B-2 bombers.

Washington Helps Select the Site for Airfields

Because the military used them as well, it had a hand in selecting the city's airfields. In August 1925, when the city was looking at sites for an aviation field, Major Henry Miller, chief of the Militia Aviation Bureau, Washington, D.C. inspected two properties – the proposed sites for an aviation field near Nashville.

The sites being considered were the newly opened McConnell Field on Murphy Road and the Blackwood Field tract on Lebanon Road, which was 2.7 miles from the Nashville Post Office. The Major preferred the Lebanon Road site because "the distance was ideal and the natural topography and small amount of work required to put it in a serviceable condition as well as the lower asking prices was in its favor." Consequently, Blackwood Field became the city's official field, and the Tennessee Air National Guard's 105th Observation Squadron remained at Blackwood Field.

Two years later, on November 29, the first of two steel hangars was transferred from Blackwood Field to McConnell Field. The following Feb. 2, 1928, Lt. John Gardner, U.S. Army Air Service and instructor of the 105th Observation Squadron, landed at McConnell Field and in ceremonies there, made that field the squadron's official site.

Nashville's McConnell Field played a key role in the historic first airmail and passenger flight in December 1928. It would continue to serve the community as the city's main airfield in the 1920s.

Among the famous to have flown from McConnell field was aviatrix Amelia Earhart, who would become the first woman to fly solo across the Atlantic in 1932. Earhart spent a week in Nashville in 1931 giving flying lessons at the Hap Hazard School of Flying located at McConnell Field. Jim Fulbright writes in Aviation in Tennessee that Earhart "thrilled many local people with joy rides" during this week. Four years later Earhart would become the first woman to fly solo from Hawaii to California. Later, she would disappear over the Pacific in an around-the-world attempt in 1937.

Soon, McConnell Field was too small for the Army's huge bombers and fast pursuit planes to land there. Nor could the "commodious airliners" with a load of 24 passengers land there. Because McConnell Field was too small for safety, the 105th Observation Squadron couldn't use the field. Nashville's aviation pioneer leaders saw the need for a safe field that would handle present-day needs as well as future needs made necessary by advances in flying equipment.

McConnell Field's location in Nashville's suburbs and the hills surrounding the field also caused weather problems for Interstate Airlines. The airline bought land in nearby Rutherford County in early 1929 and construction began on Sky Harbor, June 5 that year that would accommodate larger commercial planes. McConnell Field was gradually abandoned after this Sky Harbor near Murfreesboro was completed. (McConnell Field was closed in 1937 after Berry Field opened and the land was redeveloped as the McCabe Park and Golf Course.)

Enter Sky Harbor Airport

Nashville's aviation adventure took a turn southward when Sky Harbor Airport was built halfway between Smyrna and Murfreesboro on U.S. Hwy. 41.

With pennants flying and planes zooming, crowds flocked in as the new 188-acre Sky Harbor Airport was dedicated on Oct. 14, 1929. Tennessee Governor Henry Horton and other officials and pilots with Interstate Airlines participated in the grand opening. Also among those in attendance was Wiley Post, the one-eyed pilot who reluctantly yelled a gruff "hello" into the microphone. (This pioneer American aviator would become the first person to make a solo flight around the world in July 1933, covering 15,596 miles in seven days, 18 hours and 49 minutes in a Lockheed Vega named Winnie Mae. He and the famed humorist Will Rogers were killed when a plane piloted by Post crashed in Alaska in 1935.)

The same year Sky Harbor opened, informal talks were under way for moving the 105th Squadron from McConnell Field to Sky Harbor. The military preferred to stay in Nashville because Sky Harbor was so far away from the city. But McConnell Field could only be used for training and not service planes. So the military was considering other options while waiting for action to be taken on a $250,000 Nashville bond issue to enlarge McConnell Field so it could be used by both types of aircraft. During the interim, Adjutant General W. C. Boyd did give permission for O-11 military planes to use Sky Harbor for flying maneuvers as a temporary training measure.

On Nov. 15, 1930, the adjutant general issued orders to move the 105th from Nashville to Memphis. Militia Bureau Chief General W.G. Everson ordered the 105th to meet the requirements to locate at an A-1-A airport (one available to all aircraft day and night), and there were only two others in the state besides Sky harbor – the Memphis Municipal Airport and Chattanooga's Lovell Field. The squadron disbanded in Nashville and reorganized in Memphis. All its airplanes and equipment were sent to Memphis Municipal Airport. Alas, Memphis didn't have the proper facilities available, and the program to supply them was tied up in politics.

General Everson threatened to remove the squadron from the state unless proper facilities were provided immediately. So, in March 1931, the squadron was officially transferred back to Nashville but based at Sky Harbor. The squadron would remain based there until Berry Field opened in 1937.

Financially, Sky Harbor was unsuccessful. "Those were the bond issue days of aviation and everybody talked aviation and flew, except the paying passengers," the Banner reported on June 13, 1937. Sky Harbor, with its border lights, roof-gardened club house and steel hangar, was more like a "country club," the article continued. The airport struggled while it was under the Aviation Corporation and later was swallowed up by its business-like successor, American Airlines. American then was one of the two major airlines serving Nashville.

In 1934, Postmaster General James A. Farley cancelled all airmail contracts and the Civil Aeronautics Administration began regulating airmail rates. After this airmail contract shake-up, Nashville acquired its second airline service, Eastern Airlines on June 1, 1934, and the airline map was modified. American became the airmail operator along the route from Cleveland to Los Angeles and Eastern operated over the route from Chicago to Miami. Somewhat later, American received the contract to fly mail from Washington to Nashville and along its transcontinental lanes. It was the first airmail and express service over part of the new route. Since then, passenger service was established along all routes converging at Nashville.

American flew its passengers and mail on Curtiss Condors and Ford Tri-Motors. Eastern chose Pitcairns, DC-2s and, later, Lockheed Electras, to transport mail and passengers. Both American and Eastern continued to operate from Sky Harbor until the Nashville Municipal Airport opened in 1937.

Commercial air service continued to develop nationally. Next came night flying, regular 24-hour schedules, and increasingly larger and more luxurious planes to serve passengers. With improved equipment came faster and faster schedules.

The City Outgrows McConnell Field and Sky Harbor

The need for a new airport for the city dated back to the early 1930s when city officials recognized the inadequacies of both McConnell Field and Sky Harbor. On Dec. 12, 1934, the Tennessean reported:

> The City of Nashville has one airport controlled by the city with 1,600 foot runways in two directions. This field (McConnell Field) has been declared inadequate for scheduled airline operations. It has one hangar, telephone and mechanical service, filling station and taxi service. It has no lighting equipment for night flying. It is used exclusively for the private flying and some schoolwork.
>
> Sky Harbor, the field, which is used by the airlines that serve Nashville, is located 24 miles southeast of Nashville and seven miles northwest of Murfreesboro. This field is owned by the American Airlines, Inc. Its shape is somewhat similar to a triangle whose longest dimension is 3,000 feet and its shortest 1,950 feet. It is sodded and has natural drainage.

The field is day marked and is completely lighted for night flying. Facilities at this airport consist of mail, passenger and express service, weather bureau, radio station, filling station, administration building, hangar, telephone, etc. The 105th Observation Squadron of the Tennessee National Guard is located at Sky Harbor.

Although the field at Sky Harbor was lighted, when fog engulfed the airfield at night (as it often did), pilots had to fly to another landing site. Sky Harbor lacked the space to expand and all-weather instrument runways to meet demand.

By now, American was already flying the DC-2 and an even bigger plane (the DC-3) was in the planning stage. Clearly, Nashville needed a new airfield.

Two years later, the Nashville Banner on June 13, 1937 – the day the new airport opened – recapped the building of the new airport and also recounted the need for this new airport. The article noted that this need for modern ground facilities for fliers had been "long realized by scores of forward-looking citizens of Nashville."

The 105th Observation Squadron members led the way. Blackwood Field, near the Hermitage on Lebanon Pike, was "outmoded almost from the start." McConnell Field had "many limitations." After McConnell, the airlines and the squadron used Sky Harbor (which was 24 miles from Nashville). While it was a vast improvement and "served well for a time the needs of progressive Murfreesboro and the ever-growing Capital City, it, too, soon proved to be inadequate and inconvenient, as aviation made rapid strides."

The Banner identified one of the chief proponents of the new airport as the Junior Chamber of Commerce, which joined with other air-minded citizens.

One reason Nashville needed a new airport, according to the Banner, was the city's strategic location, commercially, geographically and defensively – especially defensively. While an airport in Nashville would provide a facility of great commercial value in peace, it would be of immense value in case of war. Furthermore, the project could put hundreds of men to work under the Works Progress Administration (WPA) program.

The WPA was part of President Franklin Delano Roosevelt's New Deal, designed to help the nation recover from the Great Depression.

Although Mayor Hilary Howse and other community and business leaders realized the need for a new airport, many citizens were less enthusiastic. Nashville and the rest of the country were just beginning to recover from the Depression. The city had to turn elsewhere to find help in getting the airport built.

The Tennessee WPA Airport Program came to the rescue. The U.S. Bureau of Air Commerce also arranged for matching construction funds from those communities requesting help. The Tennessee WPA helped build five first-class airports and seven landing fields. One of those fields was Berry Field in Nashville.

Choosing a Site for a Municipal Flying Field

On Feb. 6, 1935, the Tennessean reported that Colonel John B. Wynne of the Department of Commerce in D.C. had advised the Nashville Airport Committee "to make all preparations for building a local municipal flying field and to be 'ready to shoot' on the first proposition in the way of financial aid offered by the federal government."

The article noted that all but two members of the 14-member committee asked by Mayor Howse to meet to discuss ways to purchase and build an airport were present at the February 5 meeting. The group voted to make the mayor's Airport Advisory Committee permanent and selected Will Cheek, representing the Nashville Chamber of Commerce, as chairman. (Cheek's family was in the wholesale grocery business. A relative, Joel Cheek, founded the Cheek-Neal Coffee Company and created the world famous Maxwell House blend of coffee.)

"At the outset of the meeting," the article reported, "Mayor Howse reviewed the history of Nashville's airports, declaring 'Nashville needs a class A airport, I know, and city officials are most interested in the project.'"

Chairman Cheek, in turn, appointed a site selection subcommittee that included local banker and Nashville aviation pioneer Colonel Herbert Fox, Tennessean receiver L. J. Pardue and Banner publisher James G. Stahlman.

Colonel Wynne agreed to stay in Nashville for several days to help in site selection. The site selection subcommittee, along with Wynne, the next day began touring prospective sites. In all, they studied and graded eight possible sites before recommending one to the full committee on June 25, 1935. The committee unanimously accepted the subcommittee's recommendation and on November 6 that year, the Nashville City Council approved legislation authorizing the city to acquire the property in question.

The Nashville Banner on June 13, 1937, also had reviewed how the site was selected. The article noted that the first consideration was for a safe field. The second was cost and convenience. With that in mind, the site selection subcommittee had ruled out sites too close to the city's smoke and manufacturing plants for safety reasons. Other sites were too close to residential areas, railroads and other hazards. They also carefully checked all areas for fog, smoke, drainage, traffic lanes and distance from the post office. Local pilots, engineers from the Bureau of Air Commerce in D.C., engineers from the airlines were all consulted.

The final choice was made. The winning site was on Murfreesboro Pike, just six miles from downtown with only one 90-degree traffic turn in that six-mile stretch. That meant those airmail runs to the post office could safely be made in 20 minutes. The 337-acre site encompassed four farms.

More precisely, the site for the new airport was located between Murfreesboro Road and Stones River Road and Bogle Road (now Hangar Lane) and McGavock Lane.

Nashville businessman Nelson Andrews recalled that his grandfather assembled the land for the planned airport and it was almost named for him. This didn't happen because of another person who played a key role in the development of the new airfield. This person was Colonel Harry S. Berry, state administrator of the Tennessee-Works Progress Administration (WPA) Airport Program and a native of Hendersonville, Tenn.

Works Progress Administration to the Rescue!

Before the Depression took its toll, Nashville had enjoyed great economic growth. Thanks to its banks and investment companies, the city ranked at the front of American financial centers. This growth and prosperity went hand in hand with a transportation boom. Planes, trains and automobiles contributed to the city's status as a regional trade center. Forty passenger trains a day carried commuters to outlying towns in Middle Tennessee.

The Depression brought all this growth to an abrupt standstill. So, when President Roosevelt's New Deal offered Nashville and the nation a helping hand, the city grabbed hold and worked with the federal government to recover from this economic quagmire.

The federal government invested approximately $16,000,000 in Tennessee under the WPA. Among the beneficiaries were Memphis, Knoxville, Chattanooga, Crossville, Kingsport, Johnson City, Bristol and Nashville.

The purpose of the WPA was twofold: (1) to provide honorable work for the men temporarily out of private employment and (2) to provide the public with lasting, useful improvements.

Federal funds helped build a new post office, state supreme court and other state buildings and a new courthouse for the city. The WPA also provided funds for construction and improvements in Edwin and Percy Warner Parks.

More importantly, Nashville would get a much-needed new airport from the program.

The Magic Transformation Begins

The Nashville Banner's recap of the construction of the new airport reported that engineers had to overcome many problems during the 18 months it took to complete the project. Massive excavation was required to reshape the topography, leveling the peaks of hills and filling valleys and gullies spreading out and pounding down to turn 337 acres of rugged farmland into a new municipal airport. This earth had to be covered with a gigantic "X" of asphaltic concrete. When completed, the new facility would include three runways and five buildings (municipal hangar, the administration building, hangar for the 105th Observation Squadron plus an administration building and drill hall for the Squadron).

While the city made plans for this new airport, airlines were making plans for transatlantic service and Nashville was included in these plans.

On March 15, 1936, the Nashville Banner reported that "the Nashville Municipal Airport will be the terminus of a feeder line leading to Charleston, start of the Pan American Airlines' proposed transatlantic service air officials now consider definite." A map showed "the position of the Nashville field in relation to those from the Lake and Western States." Also included was a photo of the final field plans for the Nashville Airport. Included on the drawing were the new runways and the five buildings and hangars to be located along Bogle Road.

The article also reported that more than 46 acres of concrete would be poured in creating the hard surface for the three runways and the taxi strip. A Works Progress Administration (WPA) allotment of $380,000 had been made for the field. Colonel Berry had asked for another grant of $250,000. The administration building and hangar nearest Murfreesboro Road would be for municipal use. The other hangar, the assembly hall, and the drill hall were to be used by the 105th Observation Squadron.

Colonel Berry told the Tennessean in April 1936 that the total expenditure for the new modern A-1 airport in Nashville, when completed and put into service about May 15, 1937, "will be right at $1,190,000, including federal and city funds."

A couple of months later on June 24, 1936, an American Airlines DC-2 became the first airplane to land at the new airport, (Berry Field) which was still under construction. Airport officials and civic leaders hopped on board for short flights around the field in this preview event.

That fall the city began planning for dedication ceremonies under the direction of Nashville Municipal Airport committee chairman Will Cheek. Seven subcommittees were appointed to coordinate the festive events surrounding the dedication on November 1. The 105th Observation Squadron, which was planning a flying show to climax dedication exercises, claimed it would be the "most spectacular air event in this city's history." Included in the plans was an aerial parade of approximately 100 military and privately owned planes circling over Nashville before flying to the new airport and landing there for the public to inspect before the afternoon's air show.

Nashville Dedicates its New Airport

The dedication of the new airport on Nov. 1, 1936, was another red-letter day in Nashville's aviation adventure.

The city at the time the new airport was dedicated, was anticipating the upcoming presidential election on November 11 in which Democratic incumbent Franklin D. Roosevelt was facing Republican challenger Governor Alf Landon. Shirley Temple was the darling of the box office and her latest film "Dimples" was showing at the Paramount Theater. The Tennessean sports page that day reported "Tennessee Buries Georgia Bulldogs under 46 to 0 Defeat with Great Exhibition" while "Vandy Mistakes Help Powerful L.S.U. to Gain 19-0 Triumph."

Cain Sloan advertised three-piece, women's genuine Lustratone suits for $49.95 and permanent waves for $5. Car dealers touted the 1937 models of Chryslers, Pontiacs, Plymouths, Buicks, Nashes, Chevrolets, Fords, Dodges and Studebakers. Those headed for the big event at the new airport no doubt drove these American-made cars as they ventured out to participate in the festivities.

The city unveiled an elaborate traffic plan to handle those planning to attend the dedication festivities. Two-lane Murfreesboro Road was made one-way and closed to all cars except those headed for the airport event. Through traffic was re-routed to Nolensville, Lebanon and Franklin Pikes and Old Hickory Boulevard (I-40 didn't exist at the time.)

The mass aerial parade over the city, the firing of aerial bombs during the national anthem, formation flying and military maneuvers by six military planes, high speed acrobatic flying by the Sky Hawks team and crazy flying maneuvers by Capt. Dick Granere titled "How Not To Fly" entertained the crowds.

Also part of the festivities was the record breaking parachute jump but not from the altitude of 20,000 feet as previously reported by the 105th's Major Walter Williams in the Tennessean (Oct. 8, 1936). This most daring feat of its type ever attempted was possibly too daring because another report noted the parachute jump by Bob O'Dell from St. Louis was from a 10,000-foot altitude.

Reportedly, a giant American Airlines plane "swooped" down to pick up a consignment of "special cachet 'airmail.'" The plane was the first regular mail plane to leave the field.
Local, state and national dignitaries attending included:

Will T. Cheek, general chairman of the Nashville Airport dedication committee and chairman of the permanent airport committee of the Chamber of Commerce. (Later in June 1937, an advertisement in the Official Program saluted Cheek, noting his "vision and untiring efforts as head of the Nashville Airport Committee were largely responsible for the successful outcome of this project.")

Mayor Hilary E. Howse, who formally accepted the airport from Colonel Harry S. Berry, state WPA administrator;

Colonel Harry S. Berry of the WPA who led the effort to build the new airport;

C.R. Smith, president of American Airlines, who flew in from headquarters in Chicago in a powerful new 32-passenger Douglas plane;

Captain Eddie Rickenbacker, American flying ace and leader of the famous 94th "Hat in the Ring" squadron of the A.E.F. air service and vice president and general manager of Eastern Airlines;

Major General Frank M. Andrews "Hometown boy" and commander of the General Headquarters Air Corps for the U.S. Army; and

Major James Doolittle, a pioneer in blind flying (he was the first to take off and land a plane solely by the reading of the instruments on the dashboard on Sep. 24, 1929).

An Airport for the People

An excited crowd of 40,000 people had gathered on or near the new airfield for the dedication ceremonies in November and that same number returned eight months later, on June 12-13, 1937, when Berry Field opened. Reportedly, Wesley Dyer was the pilot of the first plane to take off from Berry Field.

The project had cost the city $144,227 and the federal government $1,039,937 for a total of $1,184,164. The new municipal field, built jointly by the WPA and the City of Nashville, was within quick distance of the heart of the business district and occupied 337 acres.

Saturday's opening festivities included a parade of planes downtown and a sky parade over Nashville plus an aviation banquet, aviation ball and even a simulated mock "bombing" of Nashville by the 105th Aero Squadron.

Sunday's events included brief addresses by officials, including Tennessee Governor Gordon Browning. Also part of the day's festivities was the arrival and departure of Eastern Airlines and American Airlines planes from and to various cities along with assorted parachute jumps, wing-walking demonstration, mid-air refueling demonstration and a mile-high double wedding in an American Airlines plane to name just a few.

The Reverend J.D. Hewgley, a Methodist minister, presided at this double wedding as Miss Frances Meadows and P.W. Cox and Miss Ella Lee Smith and Herman Drake said their "I dos" in the aircraft as it flew above the new airfield. The two couples were dressed all in white (suits for the men and long, straight skirts and jackets for the women). The brides carried matching bouquets and wore duplicate hats. All four, sporting neckties to complete their wedding ensembles, made brief radio speeches before and after the ceremony.

Festivities were to culminate with the Honorary Cordell Hull, Secretary of State, turning on the field lights from Washington, D.C., through facilities of the Postal Telegraph Co., but he had to decline participation, so Nashville Public Works board member Luther Luton did the honors at 8 p.m. on Sunday. Two hours later, an American Airlines DC-3 made the first night landing. This Douglas Sleeper Transport was only the sixth built by the McDonald Douglas Company and was on its maiden transcontinental voyage. The American Airlines plane stopped in Nashville long enough for Miss Nancy Berry, daughter of Colonel. Harry Berry, to christen the flagship "The Tennessee."

Earlier in the afternoon, an Eastern Airlines plane made the first scheduled landing at the new field when it stopped for five minutes before continuing its flight from Miami to Chicago.

Although the day's ceremonies marked the official opening, regular daily airline service did not begin until July as officials completed the installation of radio equipment and building fixtures.

The three-story terminal building, located on the east side of the field, featured waiting rooms, ticket offices, postal and telegraph offices, a weather bureau, restrooms and administrative office space. The 10-foot wide glassed in control tower and an observation deck topped the terminal building.

A Model Airport for the Nation

In that Nashville Banner article on June 13, the WPA, which built five airports in Tennessee, declared "the field in Nashville is regarded as a model for the nation." Pilots could see the entire runway assigned to them thanks to the level grading. Attention was paid to proper drainage. The runways were laid out after a careful study of the prevailing winds. One ran in a southwest-northeast direction and one in a southeast-northwest line. Both were 4,000 feet paved with additional turf for emergency use. The 3,300-foot-long crossbar lay practically east and west. Both runways and the crossbar were 150-feet wide to accommodate the largest aircraft in existence. Trees were topped and some removed; telephone and power lines were moved back and a lighting system of the latest design was installed to light the field at night. The new field had a controllable searchlight of nearly a million and a half candlepower to guide planes in.

The new field – with its two paved runways and crossbar, soon to be followed by an all-weather radio beam for landings by instrument control – meant that Nashville had an airport that was a credit to the city.

This new Nashville Airport, rated as one among 23 outstanding new airports in the country, was prepared to service Eastern Air Lines and American Airlines. Through ads in the opening's Official Program, Eastern promised "luxurious 'club-car' comfort. No dust. No flickering shadows or unpleasant joggling" in its giant skyliners. American boasted of its flagship skysleepers and high speed Douglas Airliners and "planes air-cooled by nature all the way."

The WPA's Colonel Berry wrote in the opening day program of the "travel opportunities which this airport offers to the public and which makes Nashville a primary air transportation center." He continued, "It has been the constant aim of the WPA to concentrate its efforts and its resources on projects of permanent social and economic value and this airport which we put into service today is to an outstanding degree one of that character."

When Berry Field opened in 1937, an article in the Official Program by Burr Cullom proclaimed that "Nashville is fast becoming an air center" and went on to dub the city as "the Southern Cross Roads of the Air." He discussed the city's cultural, commercial, industrial and defensive importance and what the new airport meant in these areas. "Thanks to air travel, the city is now only a few hours' flight from the coast, and therefore figures into the defensive needs of the country," Cullum said.

He also discussed the work that went into building the new airport and described the features it boasted, including the three-story high administration building and two fireproof hangars. He noted that, "it is believed that the Bureau of Air Commerce will in the near future install an all-weather radio beam for landings by instrument control." And he described how the Nashville Iris Society planned to plant masses of various colored irises to identify Nashville as "The Iris City." Included in the plans was a 300-foot long and 12-foot wide planting of thousands of blooms depicting the "spread-wings" emblem of the air pilot. This would be visible from the air and ground.

Later that year in a Tennessean article (Nov. 7, 1937), American Airlines President C.R. Smith described the new Nashville Airport as a "link in a chain of fields across the country contributing to the safety of commercial aviation and as a potential factor in the event of war or invasion."

Speaking during a visit to the city, Smith announced that Nashville had been selected as one of the Southern stops for the new 40-passenger planes the airline was planning to place in service the next year. He also pointed out that Nashville was on the Southern transcontinental route which, he predicted, "would likely become the heaviest-traveled in the country."

The same story reported that Will T. Cheek, chairman of the State Board of Aeronautics, and Mayor Howse were to confer on the purchase of land to enlarge the field to accommodate the new planes.

When 1937 ended, Berry Field already had served 189,000 passengers.

As early as 1940, city and county officials had taken steps to prepare a master plan for expansion at the city airport, according to the Tennessean (Sept. 28, 1940). Officials discussed planning and zoning and problems connected with expansion. Plans called for surveying an area in a three- to five-mile radius of the airport.

They turned to land on which Colonel E.W. Cole had built his home Colemere (later the Colemere Club and now a seafood restaurant) shortly after his retirement as president of the Nashville, Chattanooga and St. Louis Railroad in 1893. Late in 1940, part of this land was bought for the addition to Berry Field. The expansion of Nashville's airport would come not just to accommodate American Airlines' new planes. Nashville's strategic location, cited by C.R. Smith and Burr Cullom when the new airport opened, would come into play as the country again went to war.

The War Years — Military Management

Chapter 3

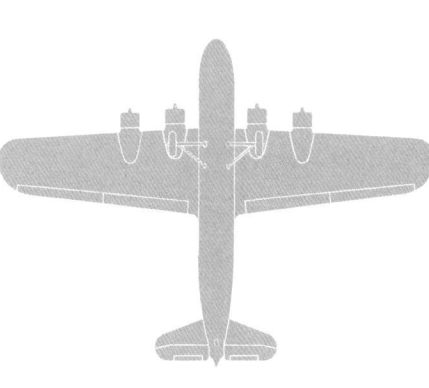

Chapter 3
The War Years—Military Management

The military played a major role in Nashville's aviation history from 1941 until 1946. During those years, the federal government operated the airport as a major military aircraft clearing station. Berry Field was home of the 4th Ferrying Command, operating as one of the country's largest clearing stations for aircraft bound for Africa, India, Italy and Egypt.

When this unit relocated to Memphis, the 20th Ferrying Group was created in Nashville. Pilots flew newly produced warplanes from production factories around the country to Berry Field. Here they were equipped for flights to front-line units.

During this time, the Air Transport Command (ATC) operated a large training facility at Nashville. ATC pilots flew the factory-fresh aircraft overseas. These ATC pilots also flew thousands of war casualty convalescent cases through Nashville daily on their journeys to reach hospitals close to their homes and families.

During the war years, the federal government added additional acreage at Berry Field for its military operations and in 1946 returned an improved airport containing 1,500 acres to the City of Nashville.

The National Guard continued to be based at the Nashville Airport in the ensuing years. The Tennessee National Guard's 105th Observation Squadron, which flew missions including reconnaissance and fighter-interceptor operations during the 1930s and 1940s, continued these operations during the 1950s. In 1961, the 105th became the flying squadron of the 118th Air Transport Wing.

John Tune, who would play a key role in the airport's future, was called up by the Air National Guard during the Korean Conflict and became a brigadier general and the chief of staff in the Tennessee Air National Guard.

Today, Nashville International remains the home of the Tennessee Air National Guard, one of the largest Air National Guard facilities in the country. The unit's airlift mission continues today as part of the 118th Airlift Wing.

"The military has been on this airport for a long, long time," recalled William G. Moore, Jr., a former four-star general of the U.S. Air Force who served as president of Nashville's Airport Authority from 1984 to early 2001.

In addition to the ferry command base here during World War II, he noted that one aircraft manufacturer has been building military aircraft adjacent to this airport since prior to World War II. Originally known as Stinson Aircraft Corporation, this company built its first plant in 1939-40 on the west side of the airfield. Its ownership and name have changed many times (Stinson, Vultee, Avco, Textron, and The Aerostructure Corp.). The plant, according to author Jim Fulbright in Aviation in Tennessee, "has produced a variety of aircraft types and parts, ranging from civilian airplanes to World War II fighters to wing structures for the C-5B," the free world's largest aircraft. In recent years, the plant produced tail sections for the Lockheed C-130 Hercules.

The military also based a wing of C-130 aircraft airlift at Nashville and provided facilities for them. (The C-130 was used to carry troops or equipment.) The local unit has been involved in most of the nation's military engagements in recent years, including the Persian Gulf War. The wing also has seen action in Bosnia, Somalia, Kosovo and Iraq.

"The modern military must react quickly, and speed is of the essence. It is important to keep in mind that most of the things that go into a military operation are flown in. So, the importance of airlift has really increased," General Moore said.

"Military and commercial flying are completely compatible at Nashville," General Moore said. They operate in a separate area across the field on the basis of a long-term lease. I expect we'll see them there for as long as the Department of Defense supports their operations here."

Nashville Debutante Becomes a Military Hero

A history of aviation in Nashville would not be complete without mentioning one of the city's great World War II heroes – Cornelia Fort.

The daughter of Dr. Rufus E. Fort, one of the founders of National Life & Accident Insurance Company, this young aviatrix spurned her life as a wealthy debutante to embrace flying. Her first flight was in a J-3 Cub from Berry Field. Exhilarated by the experience, she went on to earn a private pilot's license in June 1940 and her Instructor Certificate in just over a year after her first lesson. Nashville's first female flight instructor then taught in Colorado and Hawaii.

It was in Hawaii on the morning of Dec. 7, 1941, that this 22-year-old flight instructor and her student pilot encountered Japanese fighters flying directly at them. Fort reacted quickly and avoided a collision but watched in disbelief as this plane joined a wave of Japanese aircraft that were attacking Pearl Harbor in the distance. She landed her Interstate Cadet trainer in a rain of machine gun fire at a remote airport below.

Fort returned to the states in March 1942 and in September that year became a charter member of the Women's Auxiliary Ferrying Service (WAFS). This elite group of women pilots helped the war effort by ferrying military aircraft around the country. Cornelia Fort became the first woman pilot in U.S. history to die while on active military duty when the plane she was ferrying crashed after a mid-air collision in Texas on March 21, 1943. She was only 23 years old when she lost her life serving her country.

In 1944, Norman Thomas of Chattanooga bought 200 acres in a bend in the Cumberland River in East Nashville to build an airfield. The land was adjacent to property owned by Cornelia Fort's father, so Thomas named his field Cornelia Fort Airpark. Several owners later, this privately owned airport is still in use today by light aircraft and seaplanes, which can land on the bordering Cumberland River. This public use airport is just a couple of miles from Nashville International Airport.

Today, the military continues to play an important role along with passenger, cargo and general aviation as part of Nashville International's full-service operation.

Post World War II: City Management

Chapter 4

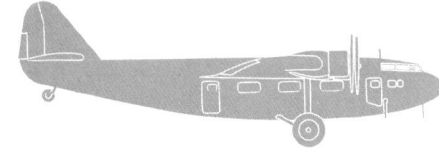

Chapter 4
Post World War II: City Management

With the exception of military management during the World War II years, the city's Department of Aviation operated the airport from the time it opened in 1937 until 1970. Its operations were subsidized annually by Nashville's taxpayers and general obligation bonds financed physical improvements.

Nashville's proximity to the nation's population centers has always played a major role in the growth and development of the city's air service. Its strategic position served as a magnet for increasing numbers of companies relocating to the city and to those that were founded and emerged to prominence here. Airlines were including Nashville in their plans long before World War II ended.

An article in the Aug. 16, 1943, edition of the Tennessean reported on American Airline's proposed transatlantic routes to London, England, following the war. Nashville was included on the direct transatlantic air routes.

Six months later on February 20, once again the Tennessean carried an illustration noting Nashville's post-war air importance due to its geographic location. The illustration outlined one-day business trips by air from Nashville to such cities as New Orleans, Atlanta, Miami, Birmingham, Memphis, Los Angeles, Oklahoma City, St. Louis, Chicago, Detroit and Washington, D.C.

Nashville's geographic location was a factor in 1957 when the federal government announced plans for 12 new aerial "super skyways," designed to handle non-stop flights between the East and West coasts. According to the Tennessean (May 9, 1957), "One of the 'super-highways' will include Nashville between Washington and Los Angeles."

"In effect, the newly designed airways would improve air safety by putting virtually all non-stop transcontinental airlines into 'controlled air space.' They would fly routes monitored by federal air traffic control centers and equipped with powerful electronic navigation aids," reported the Tennessean.

The article further reported that the system was to be put into operation as soon as high-powered navigational equipment was available and listed the target date for the entire system as November 1958.

Federal Regulation Evolves with the Growth of Aviation

These super skyways were part of the National System of Aviation. The federal government's regulation of civil aviation dated back to the Air Commerce Act of May 20, 1926. In order to improve and maintain safety standards, aviation leaders appealed to the government to pass this landmark legislation. Responsibilities for fostering air commerce, issuing and enforcing air traffic rules, licensing pilots, certifying aircraft, establishing airways and operating and maintaining aids to air navigation fell under a new Aeronautics Branch of the Department of Commerce. In 1934, the Aeronautics Branch was renamed the Bureau of Air Commerce. The Bureau, noting the increase in commercial flying, encouraged a group of airlines to establish three centers to provide air traffic control (ATC) along the airways. Two years later on July 6, 1936, Federal Air Traffic Control began when the Bureau took over the three centers at Newark, Chicago and Cleveland and began to expand the ATC system.

The Civil Aeronautics Act of 1938 created a new independent agency, the Civil Aeronautics Authority (CAA). This legislation not only transferred federal civil aviation responsibilities from the Commerce Department to this new agency, but also gave the CAA the power to regulate airline fares and to determine the routes air carriers would serve.

In 1940, President Franklin Roosevelt divided the Authority's responsibilities between two agencies, the Civil Aeronautics Administration (CAA) and the Civil Aeronautics Board (CAB). Again, both were part of the Commerce Department, however, the CAB functioned independently of the Secretary. The CAA's responsibilities included air traffic control, certifying airmen and aircraft, safety enforcement and airway development. The CAB's duties included safety rulemaking, accident investigation and economic regulation of the airlines.

The CAA assumed the added task of administering the federal-aid airport program (FAAP), which was established in 1946 by the Federal Airport Act signed into law by

President Harry S. Truman. This marked the first peacetime program of financial aid aimed exclusively at promoting development of the nation's civil airports. Federal allotments were to be matched by local funds.

All this changed when President Dwight D. Eisenhower signed the Federal Aviation Act of 1958. This Act assigned all functions relating to civil aviation to two independent agencies, the Federal Aviation Agency (FAA), which was created by this law, and the Civil Aeronautics Board (CAB), which inherited the nucleus of the organization and functions of the CAA. The CAB also was freed of its ties to the Department of Commerce. The changes basically became effective Dec. 31, 1958.

The Federal Aviation Agency was renamed the Federal Aviation Administration in 1967 and became a model agency within the new Department of Transportation (DOT) which President Lyndon Johnson had signed into law in October 1966. When the DOT began operations in April 1967, the CAB's accident investigation function was transferred to the new National Transportation Safety Board (NTSB).

When the FAA became part of the DOT, the agency had already assumed responsibilities for aviation security necessitated by the hijacking epidemic of the 1960s. In 1968, the FAA was given the power to prescribe aircraft noise standards. Two years later President Richard Nixon signed the Airport and Airway Development Act of 1970, which made the FAA responsible for safety certification of airports served by air carriers. More importantly, it put the agency in charge of a new airport aid program funded by a special Airport and Airway Trust Fund.

This Aviation Trust Fund, established under the Airport and Airway Revenue Act of 1970, was designed to provide about $11 billion over the next decade for airport and airway modernization. In addition to funds Congress might appropriate for authorized expenditures, new revenues from aviation user taxes levied by the Airport and Airway Revenue Act would go into this special trust fund.

With the help of this fund, 85 new airports were built and more than 1,000 received improvements such as new runways, new taxiways, runway extensions and instrument landing systems in the first five years following passage of the Airport and Airway Development Act.

The Nashville Airport was one of those that would benefit from the Aviation Trust Fund, but not without a struggle.

Airline Service Comes Slowly to Middle Tennessee

In 1951, 21 million passengers flew in domestic airlines within the U.S., up from six million in 1945 and just four million in 1941. People were quickly embracing flying as a mode of transportation.

Although it was a geographic center and figured into the government's super skyways system, Nashville lagged behind other cities in terms of airline service during the 1950s. According to the Tennessean on July 15, 1957, CAB examiner William J. Madden had recommended a fourth major airline to serve Nashville. Emphasizing the city's need for more North-South service, he urged National Airlines be allowed to provide service from St. Louis to Jacksonville via Nashville and Atlanta.

The editorial noted that in 1940 Nashville was 28th among airline stations in passenger ticket sales. The city dropped to 34th by 1949 and was ranked 40th in 1955.

The reason given for this decline was partly because of "lack of impetus of competitive service" and partly because "it has received almost no air coach service."

The article further noted that business, civic and political leaders were making continuous efforts to promote better air service and added "it's long been inconvenient to reach some points from Nashville without needless rerouting."

The city was on the threshold of the "jet age" in terms of a greatly expanded municipal airport, the newspaper report continued. "The airport has longer runways and larger and more complete terminal operation facilities, but it is not going to share in that age much without expanded service. The lack of added service, the editorial predicted, "will be costly in terms of negotiations for new industry and in terms of tomorrow's demand for air transportation and cargo, costly in terms of commerce lost to us." The Tennessean called Nashville's struggle an "inch-by-inch" one.

This struggle for added service during an era of regulation would soon find the city appealing to the Civil Aeronautics Board in Washington, D.C. The Tennessean reported in December 1957 that the city was involved in four cases before the CAB in which five major airlines were "offering to provide service links with other cities to get new, improved and competitive service from both major and feeder airlines."

One of these cases was the St. Louis-Southeast Service Case, under consideration since February 1957. The Civil Aeronautics Board had intervened in this case and denied Nashville's bid. The city's special counsel Lawrence Dortch of Waller, Davis and Lansden, would, in turn, on Nov. 29, 1958, ask for a review of the CAB's decision by the federal court in Washington, D.C.

Since its creation in 1940, the CAB had explicit authority to develop competitive air transportation in this country by conducting investigations and public hearings. The President of the United States appointed the five independent board members who, in turn, were responsible to the Congress as they awarded routes. Political interests often were a factor in the CAB's decisions. This federal agency increasingly came under attack for delays in awarding air service due to a steadily increasing backlog of cases pending before it.

Chief among critics of the CAB was Nashville Mayor Ben West, who called for the abolishment of the CAB at a meeting of the American Municipal Association (AMA) in December 1957 in San Francisco. Although it deleted West's call for abolishment, the organization voted to condemn the CAB for its failure to provide cities with adequate air service and called for a congressional investigation of the federal board.

The Tennessean on Dec. 1, 1957, reported that Tennessee Senators Estes Kefauver and Albert Gore agreed to join with Congressman J. Carlton Loser to ask for an investigation of the failure of the CAB to provide Nashville with better air service.

The headline on an editorial in the newspaper that same day read, "We Are Tired of Excuses As Substitutes for Service." The editorial laments, "In spite of the fact that Nashville is at the crossroads of two of the busiest highways of the sky…the Civil Aeronautics Board up in Washington just doesn't seem to want to believe it. Every time Nashville asks the CAB to let some of these overhead travelers stop so people from this region can get aboard or land, the CAB stuffs cotton in its ears or replies with, 'Wait a while.'"

The editorial also cites all the features Nashville Airport has to offer, such as a new control tower, land to expand and a planned $3 million terminal and a new 10,000-foot runway also in the planning stages.

At the time, three major (or trunk) airlines – American, Eastern and Braniff – and two feeder (or local) lines – Ozark and Southeast – served Nashville. Chartered carriers Capitol Airways and Nashville Flying Service provided additional service.

Airline Strikes Temporarily Disrupt Service

A rash of airline strikes in 1958 compounded the city's struggle to add service. Capitol Airlines was shut down from October 17 to November 22 by a mechanics strike. TWA flights were grounded when 6,700 machinists went out on strike November 22-30. Eastern also was shut down on November 24 when 5,500 members of the International Machinists Union and 600 flight engineers walked off the job, striking in support of improvements in wages and working conditions. The engineers also objected to the company's proposal that they take basic pilot training for service on jet airliners, which were to go into service in 1960.

Some 1,500 American pilots and co-pilots walked off the job on December 19 and 20,000 of the airline's other employees were furloughed without pay. The pilots were striking because the airline decided to hire mechanic-trained flight engineers to fill the third seat on the Boeing 707 despite a Presidential Emergency Board's recommendation that flight engineers on jetliners should have training to qualify for a commercial pilot's certificate.

Both Eastern and American settled their strikes and resumed flights in early January after the airlines agreed to add a third pilot to the 707 cockpit and increase the crew number to four.

Despite the uncertainty posed by the threat of these strikes, Nashville had cause to remain optimistic. Some of the city's efforts to add service paid off. The Banner had reported on Dec. 10, 1958, the addition of the first international airline to Nashville after a three-year fight. In making the announcement, Charles S. Thomas, president of Trans World Airlines, praised the teamwork of Mayor Ben West's Aviation Commission, the Chamber of Commerce Aviation Committee and civic leaders. Thanks to this teamwork, Thomas said, TWA added "another great business center to the airline system."

For the first time, long range jet stream and Super G Constellations began flying into and out of Nashville on December 16 and December 17 – the 55th anniversary of the Wright brothers' first flight. Shortly, Boeing 707s and Convair 880s were to be added to the fleet. The two TWA flights daily gave Nashville service to L.A., San Francisco and St. Louis to the West, and Atlanta, Tampa-St. Petersburg/Clearwater, and Miami in the Southeast.

This meant improved service for pleasure travel plus expansion in industry and commerce. The article noted, "Thomas called the jet age the greatest revolution in civilian travel since the dawn of mankind."

Shortly after TWA's arrival in Nashville, Banner City Hall columnist Dick Battle wrote about the additional air service.

"Nashville is winning its strong fight for more air service and more airlines and the benefits of that resolute and continuing effort by many men never have been more dramatically demonstrated than during the past few weeks," he wrote on Jan. 7, 1959.

Battle noted that when strikes forced Eastern and American to halt service, Nashville air passengers had three others to take up the slack and a big fourth (TWA) on the way. Chartered services Capitol Airways and Nashville Flying Service had joined the other major airlines to fill the need for additional service while Eastern and American were on strike. "Two years ago," the reporter reminded readers, "strikes would have virtually stranded air passengers." In contrast, now Braniff had been in Nashville for almost two years, Southeast for about a year and Ozark since about 1954. "TWA came in three weeks ago," he wrote. Nashville had come a long way in a few short years from only two to six airlines.

Battle also cited Mayor Ben West's fight for more air service, which dated back to his earliest days in office, beginning seven years previously. Battle credited Mayor West with originating the idea of an Aviation Commission. He pushed the plan through and enlisted services of Air Force Reserve Brigadier General Frank T. McCoy, recognized nationally as one of the best informed men in the aviation field. This Aviation Commission, the Chamber of Commerce's Aviation Committee and West's determination were key factors in this gradually successful fight for more air service, a fight to make Nashville the "air center of the South."

"We're not teamed up with any one airline," West said. "We are a friend to all of them. We'll go after any line that can give Nashville more and better service and we'll ask, petition and argue for more service from the lines we've got. The point we make is that we want the SERVICE." Finally, the column concludes, the city at the time was pushing for needed service to the North (Chicago, Detroit and Pittsburgh) and to the South (Birmingham Pensacola, Biloxi, Gulfport and New Orleans).

Finally, Battle again mentioned the city's bid through the cases in federal court and also mentioned a new $3 million terminal. The city had begun planning for this new airport terminal in 1958.

City leaders knew that the airport must provide adequate facilities in order to serve additional airlines. When an Eastern Lockheed Electra ushered in the jet age with the first jet service to Nashville in 1960, the airport was getting ready for this next stage in aviation history.

Opening a New "Jet Age" Terminal

Thousands turned out for a sneak preview of the city's new $4.5 million jet age passenger terminal on Sunday, Oct. 22, 1961, although the "official" open house and dedication festivities were set for October 28-29.

On that weekend, Saturday's visitors could take a 30-minute "flightseeing" trip around the city in a DC-6 for just $4.95 per passenger. On Sunday, American Airlines had a Boeing 707 Astrojet parked at the terminal for visitors to inspect. Eastern had a Super Electra propjet on exhibit.

Mayor Ben West and other city officials formally opened the Municipal Airport's jet age terminal on Wednesday, Nov. 1, 1961, the 25th anniversary of the dedication of the Nashville Municipal Airport at Berry Field on Nov. 1, 1936. Dr. Oren A. Oliver, chairman of the Aviation Commission, helped with the ribbon cutting and handed a gold master key to Mayor West who, in turn, handed it to James W. Hooper, general superintendent of the city's Department of Aviation, and airport manager.

American Airlines flight 628 from Los Angeles, Dallas and Memphis, was the first aircraft to use the new facilities. The plane taxied up to the new terminal at 2:30 a.m. and departed at 3 a.m. for Washington and New York. Even earlier, local pilot Ernest Colbert of Colemill Flying School flew a Piper Commanche from Cornelia Fort Airpark to the new airport at five minutes past midnight on Wednesday to be the first aircraft to land at the field after it was put into service.

During the weeklong festivities that preceded the opening, Mayor West called the new terminal "Nashville's entry into the jet age," and added, "it is the nation's finest inland airport – Nashville's dramatic port of entry for new business, industrial expansion and broadening economic horizons."

Also as part of the preliminary events, Federal Aviation Administrator Najeeb E. Halaby was guest speaker at a dedication dinner attended by 850 guests in the new terminal lobby on October 24. In his speech, the FAA chief predicted that Nashville's airport would see 200,000 operations per year by 1971. Halaby, who had flown the first jet plane to land in Nashville in 1945 while a Navy test pilot, praised the airport terminal. He also lauded the farsightedness of the city in its concept of an airport-complex and planning for new businesses to locate in the industrial development portion of the airport. (Shoe and apparel manufacturing and retail firm Genesco had already announced plans to build its new world headquarters on part of the 500 acres of airport property set aside for industrial development.)

Those attending opening events could tour the facility with its 192,340 square feet of floor space – 145,000 of which were being utilized at the time of the opening. Located on the west side of the airfield, the new west terminal building featured two concourses that could accommodate 14 parked aircraft at one time, compared to six at the old terminal. (Should future traffic warrant it, both concourses could be extended to accommodate 22 parked aircraft.)

Designed by architects Donald F. Steinbaugh & Associates of Nashville, the building had three floors with room to add four more floors later if necessary.

Department passengers unloaded baggage under a covered canopy and walked directly into the ticketing area with airline check in counters located in a single long row for convenience. From there, they took the escalator up to the airfield level, which featured a lobby with seating for 200 people. Both concourses were accessible from the lobby. Off the lobby was a Sky Chef restaurant and coffee shop. Arriving passengers took the north escalator down to the street-level baggage claim area and walked directly outside for ground transportation. Parking facilities for 750 cars for passengers and 250 for employees were available with the capability to expand to accommodate 2,000 vehicles.

Other features included a nursery for up to 10 youngsters, a banking facility and car rental and airline insurance counters. Space was also available for barber and beauty shops and other concessions.

A modern control tower, built by the city in 1955, was located just south of the new terminal. Fitted with approximately $3.5 million worth of state of the art electronic equipment and staffed by FAA air traffic control personnel, the tower served the Nashville Airport and instrument traffic for Sewart Air Force Base.

The Tennessee Air National Guard, its 118th Air Transport Wing and 118th Air Transport Group were headquartered at Nashville Municipal Airport.

American, Braniff, Eastern, Ozark, Southern and Trans World Airlines served Nashville at that time. Capitol Airways, the world's largest supplemental airline, was headquartered in Nashville.

A new jet runway opened during the summer prior to the terminal's opening.

The airport at this time included 2,300 areas of land situated between U.S. 41 and Interstate Route 40 (which was under construction).

When the new terminal opened, a Banner story by Dick Battle on Oct. 24, 1961, did a recap of how the airport site had been selected back in 1935. The article praised the farsightedness of the three-man subcommittee and the other members of the mayor's Airport Advisory Committee. The reporter deemed the airport site selection as key to the airport's "steady progress to become in 1961 one of the finest 'jet age' facilities in the United States."

Two years later in 1963, this growth continued as the existing runway (2L-20R) was extended by an additional 800 feet and construction began on a new runway (13-31).

Growth Creates Need for Change in Government

Nashville and Davidson County, which had experienced unprecedented growth in the 1950s, underwent a major change in government in the early 1960s.

Before World War II, the city had a mayor and a city council, while the county functioned with a county judge and a quarterly court. The separate governments had operated independently but compatibly.

The need for a unified metropolitan government arose due to divisions of inequalities between the city and county following the war. The city's population barely grew while the county's increased rapidly as more and more people moved to suburbia. This exodus from the city created a need for "city" services in the county, which didn't have resources to fund them.

Mayor Ben West and Davidson County Judge Beverly Briley tried to maintain the balance of power and did for awhile. But change was needed. After careful study and several plans for consolidation, the issue was put before the voters in 1958. Initially, the proposal was defeated. Four years later in 1962, the residents of the city and county both voted for consolidation and the two governing bodies merged.

That year, Beverly Briley was elected mayor under this new form of government, which included a 40-member Metropolitan Council. And the Metropolitan Government of Nashville and Davidson County was formally inaugurated on April 1, 1963, becoming the first consolidated city/county government in the U.S.

For the next 12 years, Mayor Beverly Briley would hold the reins to this new government, which became known simply as Metro. During this time, he sought to use this modern approach to solving urban problems as he watched the climate of the city change. Country music turned Nashville into Music City U.S.A. and gained an international following during the 1960s. Beginning in 1968, health care emerged as the largest industry in Nashville with the founding of Hospital Corporation of America.

The city and region's growth coupled with the growth of aviation during the 1960s did not go unnoticed by a group of Nashville civic leaders. This handful of visionary Nashvillians knew that aviation was an essential key to the city's and the region's future. They studied a variety of airport governance forms and borrowed the best elements of several. Through their efforts, in 1969, a development occurred that would have far-reaching and dramatic impact on the future of aviation in Middle Tennessee.

That year, Mayor Briley and the Metro Council would have to decide what to do about Nashville's airport when an equally progressive form of airport governance called an Airport Authority was proposed for Nashville and Middle Tennessee.

The New Age for Aviation Dawns in Middle Tennessee

Chapter 5

Chapter 5
The New Age for Aviation Dawns in Middle Tennessee

From its humble beginnings, aviation in Nashville and Middle Tennessee was emerging into a major force in the development of the city and region. It happened through a combination of factors: the right time, the right place and the right people. Decades before, leadership in air service had come through a coalition of city government and local business and civic activists as well as military personnel. Each had played a distinct and key role in the early governance of Nashville's airfields.

In the 1930s, when the need for a better airport surfaced, a 15-member Citizen's Airport Committee appointed by Mayor Hilary Howse did the preliminary work necessary to "secure the airport, and the members set about their work in a business-like way."

With the help of local and government pilots, engineers, aerologists, aviation engineers from Washington, D.C. and of major airlines, city officials selected a site for the new airport just six miles from the city limits of Nashville.

The City of Nashville opened Berry Field on its present site in 1937. The city continued the ownership and operation of the aviation complex until 1970, interrupted only during the 1941 to 1946 period when the federal government operated the airport as a major military aircraft clearing station. The City of Nashville owned and operated the airport through the local Department of Aviation. Nashville's taxpayers subsidized it annually; and general obligation bonds financed improvements.

According to the Colemere Handbook of City and County Government (circa 1947), Harold J. Baird was one of the mayor's administrative assistants and was designated as commissioner of aviation and public works.

Director of Aviation Col. Richard D. Gleaves, appointed by the mayor, was head of the Department of Aviation. His responsibilities included the operation, maintenance and control of the Nashville Municipal Airport, known as Berry Field, and all other airports owned in whole or in part by the city. Two divisions of the department included Berry Field and Cumberland Field; both were wholly-owned by the city.

The handbook described Berry Field as a large commercial airport serving airline traffic (passenger and freight, express and mail) and larger private aircraft as well as Army and Navy aircraft. The Fighter Squadron of the National Guard was based at Berry Field, as was the Air Reserve Group. Harold Wright was superintendent of the Berry Field Division.

Also available at Berry Field were charter services of all types and planes for sightseeing. These were operated by Base Operations, which offered repair, gas and catering service.

Cumberland Field, supervised by Superintendent Chester Borum, was located at the end of 9th Avenue North and the Cumberland River (now site of the MetroCenter complex). (This field was originally developed by businessman and pilot Jim Gillespie in 1941 when Berry Field was devoted to military use. It was an auxiliary field used by private fliers and for student instruction, both private and G.I. Also available were repair service and gas facilities for all types of small planes. The city bought the field in 1945 and changed the name from Gillespie Field to Cumberland Field. Capitol Airways co-founders Jesse Stallings and Richmond McInnis leased Cumberland Field in 1946 and operated there before later moving to Berry Field. Louis Gasser then rented this field for his Nashville Flying Service in the 1950s. Operations at the field continued into the early 1960s before the area was developed as MetroCenter.)

The city's Department of Aviation maintained the facilities of Cumberland Field and Berry Field, including maintenance of runways, lighting facilities and buildings, repairs of all types, police, porter and janitor services and many other functions but leased all facilities to the government or private concerns. The Civil Aeronautics Administration of the U.S. government supervised air traffic control.

"The Department of Aviation is self supporting from the income from rentals, which is disbursed within a budget approved by the City Council," the handbook noted.

Airport governance remained under the city's control even after Nashville and Davidson County adopted the Consolidated Government of Metropolitan Nashville (Metro) form of government in 1962.

In the ensuing years, however, a handful of citizens, led by John C. Tune, attorney, businessman, pilot and civic leader, began the process of creating a new form of governance for the airport.

Tune is remembered throughout the community as the driving force behind the development of air service and the establishment of an airport that was owned and operated independently from local government. The picture painted of him as he charged through the process is of a visionary who was capable of concepts within a bold vision. John Tune was one who understood that the devil was in the details and didn't mind looking the devil in the eye, and one who had the capacity to bring people of diverse interests together in the common pursuit of excellence in aviation. In a very real sense, the Metropolitan Nashville Airport Authority is John C. Tune's story.

Establishing the Need for a New Form of Governance

"Around about 1968 or 1969, not too long after I joined the Chamber, John Tune was chairman of the Chamber's aviation committee," Eddie Jones recalled. "He had the thought that if Nashville was going to improve its air service and facilities, that an Airport Authority was the only way to get that done!

"Up until that point the airport was a department of metropolitan government, just like the water and sewer department or public works," Jones continued. "The airline decision-makers were showing more and more reluctance to do business with, contract with and negotiate with politicians and councils and government entities. John felt like control and management of the airport should be vested in a group of business leaders who understood the airline side of things as well as the airport itself."

Pat Wilson recalled that John Tune was "disgusted with the politics" in the community and that is what prompted him to start this push for an Airport Authority. "He wanted the Authority to be free of politics and run like a business and have its own financing," said Wilson, who began with Tune as a member of the first MNAA Board of Commissioners. Wilson would go on to serve for a total of 19 years, including a term as chairman.

Robert Mathews concurred with Wilson that John Tune's unique concept was based on a need to get Nashville's aviation system out of politics. However, this wasn't the only reason.

"Air travel was no longer a luxury as it had been in the forties and fifties. In the sixties, it was the way to travel. It replaced trains. Somehow we had to figure out how to make it work. We had to think about it as a business," Mathews stressed.

He believes it would be impossible to say what actually inspired John Tune, but he thinks that Tune "realized the future of the city was its air service and its connection to the outside world. He realized the air system was going to change. It had been a luxury for wealthy people. It was about to become an essential, dominant system in moving people and goods from point A to point B. If you want to go there and get back quickly, it was essential that you be able to fly. Our city understood those facts of life, as did other cities, and we became very competitive in making certain that we were ahead of the curve in every respect. No two people had more to do with that in the modern era than did John Tune and Pat Wilson. They definitely led the charge."

Carolyn Tune, John Tune's widow and perhaps the one person who had more insight into why he wanted to create an Airport Authority, recalled her husband's desire for additional air service for the region.

"The service was limited here and I think John always felt like Nashville had, because of its location, the potential of great growth. And although he didn't necessarily want it to be another Atlanta, he felt that as far as air service, because of our location, we could really be an air center and have really, really good service," she recalled.

Another reason why the Airport Authority concept came about was financial, according to Nelson Andrews. To have additional service would require additional capital, which the city didn't have, he noted.

"The basic problem we solved with an Airport Authority was the inability of the city government to accommodate the bonded indebtedness needed for a modern airport. It was massive. It meant building runways, taxiways and roads. It required designing and constructing the terminals and related facilities, including parking and lighting and the control tower. So it was a combination of necessities. The issues involved very complex financing, politics at the local, state and federal level, and the very delicate relationships between the community and the air carriers who had competing interests.

"John Tune's idea was to make it work as a business," he recalled. "We also spent time with the airlines because it was imperative that they be a part of it. And you used their promise to pay in a way as the basis for selling bonds.

"In the beginning a lot of different groups had said, 'we just have to have a modern airport.' If you're going to be a great city or even a pretty good city you have to have a modern airport, one that's functional," he explained. "And so that came from a lot of different directions. It probably came harder from the business community than any other one place. It came from the Chamber. It came from a group called Watauga, which was an informal longer-range business-planning group that was involved in community projects. As time went on the lead-time required for a major development such as the airport became extended because of the complexity of the issues and the multiple number of interests involved.

"In the real early days, if you had a plow and could plow a strip, and you could pack it down, you could put an airport most anywhere. But those days were in the distant past when John Tune began in the 1950s and 1960s to outline his plans for Nashville's airport in the modern era," Andrews explained. The city needed to take its airport from one level to the next level.

"The air field was there when we got the Airport Authority. But it didn't have the kind of runways you needed. It didn't have a terminal that was suitable in terms of space, logistics and technology. So what our city had to do was take kind of a rinky-dink airport that couldn't handle what we needed in terms of the kind of traffic we were projected to have. Almost everything needed to be stepped up a notch – security, retailing and facilities. The whole thing was just pretty small town," he recalled.

"I think at the time if the city probably had been able to have the bonded capability to have done what needed to be done, to spend the kind of money it needed, my guess is that it would have been difficult to have a separate Airport Authority," Andrews stressed. "But they didn't, and if you put down what it was going to cost and you looked at the city's limit on its bonded indebtedness, then it just couldn't happen that way. So, the answer, of course, was the Airport Authority," Andrews said.

Finally, Carolyn Tune believed part of her husband's motivation for undertaking this cause could be attributed simply to his love of flying and his love of the community.

"John started flying really early in his life," she explained. "He said that he would go to the airport and polish airplanes so he could get a chance to fly. And he also joined the National Guard as soon as he could. During the Korean War, his guard unit was activated and just as he was getting ready to get on a ship to go to Korea, they pulled him off and he went to cadet school. So he was tremendously dedicated to the Guard and so because of his dedication and that the base was at the airport, he was really involved forever with the airport. His love of flying, it was his great joy of life."

Carolyn Tune recalled that when she and John first married, the National Guard unit based in Nashville was a reconnaissance unit and the base had jets. Guard members, in order to keep current with the planes, would go out at any time and fly, landing at different military bases.

"It was kind of like having your own private jet," she said, smiling. "Pretty nice."

Her husband switched to flying C-130s when the squadron's mission changed from reconnaissance to transports. He also flew helicopters.

This love of flying fueled his interest in the airport, his widow said. Then he got involved with community affairs.

"Always, he was really dedicated to being a public servant," she recalled. She isn't sure but guessed that her husband, because he really knew more about aviation, got started with the idea of an Authority through his involvement with the Chamber's aviation committee.

"And then he realized that it would be such a great asset to Nashville for us the taxpayers not to have to pay taxes to keep the airport going and if you have an Authority, the airport would pay for itself," she noted. "I remember him discussing that when he was telling me basically what he was doing. So I think he just saw a great need and he had the knowledge and by that time, of course, he was practicing law and so he had both the legal knowledge and the aviation knowledge to realize that this was an important thing to do. He was just vitally interested in it."

Making a Case for an Airport Authority for Nashville

The route for creating an Airport Authority for Nashville ran through the state as well as the city governments.

"John and his committee started out drafting the legislation which would create the Airport Authority," Eddie Jones explained. "And it took two key approvals: the Tennessee General Assembly – which would do whatever the Davidson County Delegation recommended – had to authorize Metropolitan government to spin off, sell the airport. And then the Metropolitan Council had to agree to let the Airport Authority buy back from the city the airport."

The enabling legislation from the Tennessee General Assembly would have to come in the form of a local bill in the state legislature.

"So, the Davidson County Delegation of the Tennessee General Assembly was the first group that had to be sold on this," said Jones. "And John worked real hard with lunches and dinners and meetings, convincing everybody that this was the best thing for the city."

It worked. The 86th Tennessee General Assembly authorized creation of the Airport Authority under Public Chapter 174 of its Public Acts during the 1969 session.

Now this citizen's group had to sell this concept to the Metropolitan Council.

According to Jones, at the time, the airport "was not being well run. There were politics involved and patronage and purchasing and all sorts of things that were not being done along good business management lines." Change was needed. "However," he continued, "there wasn't any incentive on the part of government just to voluntarily say, 'hey, let us give you an airport.'

"Beverly Briley was the mayor and we had his support which was key, I think, to getting the council to agree to take this step," added Jones.

Also key was the support of the Chamber of Commerce.

"I guess the Chamber was the driving organization pushing to make this happen, to get it done," he continued.

Nelson Andrews agreed. "The Chamber had to be a thousand percent behind it. There just wasn't any way this was going to happen without it. The Chamber, I think, was a good Chamber at the time – and it is now. We have a very strong Chamber of Commerce in this community. The Chamber obviously said, 'this is the single most important thing by far that we can do at the time to keep our city in an upward movement in terms of economic development.'"

Andrews was president of the Chamber at the time and, in fact, served in that position for the two years during which the Airport Authority concept was being conceived and touted to state and local government.

"I spent a lot of time with John Tune and became a very close personal friend," he noted. Together and separately they talked to the political components about the political action which had to occur.

"I couldn't count the number of meetings we had with (Mayor) Beverly Briley and (Governor) Buford Ellington and all kinds of political people. What I pretty much did was what John asked me to do. He really was the leader of the effort," Andrews recalled. Although the two of them discussed what political posture they'd take, it was Tune's energy and his drive that made it happen.

"It seems smooth now but it wasn't at the time. Obviously, something like that – going through a very bumpy political process – isn't all roses. He started with it and he didn't falter. He never got discouraged. He just kept at it. And we got it done."

Andrews felt the key to Tune's success was his preparation.

"He had spent a lot of time and effort thinking this whole thing through. You could bring up almost anything and he had an answer. He really was very bright, very dedicated, very committed, but all those things didn't make him a fanatic in a sense. It just made him really prepared to talk about things," he noted.

"I can remember lots of meetings we had with Beverly Briley. Briley was a good mayor. Really, I thought one of the best mayors we've ever had and did have about as much vision as any mayor could have. And he could see what John was saying, but he had to make a political move that was maybe the biggest one under his administration. So Briley was asking lots of questions. John had the answers, pretty much. And if he didn't have them, he'd go try to find them."

Andrews didn't know how long Tune had been thinking about the Airport Authority concept but once they began the political process, the two of them together spent about a year and a half in 1968-1969. During this time, he noted, Tune used him as a sounding board, bouncing ideas off him.

"John was a very step by step, organized in his mind person," his friend and colleague recalled. "The first time we ever talked about this he said, 'we've all agreed we've got to have an airport and an Airport Authority is how I think we're going to have to do this.' He had it all laid out. He said, 'here are the people we have to convince. Here are the ways I think we can go about it. Here's the body of information we need to have to make this a convincing story.' He had reams of information. He went at it like a lawyer would, I guess. He really built a case, a very, very strong case.

"He had it laid out who ought to be on the Airport Authority," Andrews added. "So he really had it from start to finish. It was like a great lawyer building a great case that he had to try in court. That's the way he built the process."

Even those who didn't want and didn't like the idea of an Airport Authority found it difficult to counter Tune's persistence.

"It was hard to argue with him when he had all the facts."

Andrews acknowledged that he spent more time on this effort than anything else he did during his Chamber presidency because Tune felt that the Chamber's support of the project would help during talks with the governor, members of the legislature, Metro Council and whomever else was politically involved.

For those critics who questioned whether this concept would work financially, whether it was economically viable, Andrews and Tune had answers. They talked with all the airlines serving Nashville at the time to convince them they were going to have enough traffic in and out of the city to make money. The airlines, in turn, would pledge their continued service.

When they talked to various airlines, Andrews said Tune even coached him what to say.

His spiel was a Chamber of Commerce type of approach: "We cannot be a good city, a great city. We all aspire to have a great city. We don't want to be another Atlanta. We understand that. We don't want to be somebody that we're not. But in order to be a good Nashville, we've got to have a good airport. In order to do that, the present facilities won't do it. Just can't. We've got to have these new facilities."

Although he would discuss financing some, mainly Andrews talked about the kinds of businesses such as Genesco, DuPont and the big insurance, financial and publishing and retailing companies whose people traveled a lot.

"We had built the demand picture and that was kind of my pitch," he explained.

The pitch was different when they met with Mayor Briley. He wanted to know in detail what this Authority was going to look like, what was going to transpire. How it would come about. He wanted to be informed.

"I guess we met more with him than any other single politician," Andrews recalled, but that was essential. "You had to have his support to go to the governor. You had to have his support to do anything with the council. You had to have his support to let the city step back and let this happen. You have a city-owned airport you're going to transfer. That's a gutsy move on the part of the mayor and council. Then you got into the state. I don't recall it being as difficult there as we thought it might.

"Governor Ellington thought the concept made sense," Andrews recalled. "The fact that a lot of state employees traveled a good bit made it a practical idea. And the application of the concept in Tennessee's capital city had a great deal to do with his buying into the idea."

The legislature naturally had a lot of questions.

"The legislature a lot of times gets hung up on some thing that may or may not be a real big issue," Andrews recalled. "I can't remember now. We were hung up on something that didn't have much to do with it. Everything in the legislative process pretty much is a swap out, so you had some of our local legislators doing a little vote trading in some cases to make it happen. I can't remember any local legislator (and there may have been one) who didn't eventually sign on."

Carolyn Tune doesn't recall any major obstacles to the process either. But, she acknowledged, "John was a very positive person. Very, very, very positive. It was always hard to get him to discuss difficulties."

Taking His Case to the Masses

John Tune did talk at length when he utilized the media in his efforts to sell the Airport Authority concept. In an interview with the Tennesean on Dec. 14, 1969, Tune discussed the need for this new form of governance.

As chairman of the Nashville Area Chamber of Commerce's aviation committee, he pointed out that while air traffic had increased nationally by about 12 percent since 1966, Nashville's Municipal Airport had seen an increase of 23 percent during this time frame. "Last year, planes landed here at the rate of more than one a minute," the article reported.

Tune further noted that the Federal Aviation Administration had predicted in 1963 that Nashville would have about a million plane movements (landings and takeoffs) per year by 1970. However, the city had experienced 1,186,000 aircraft movements in 1967, making the FAA's prediction outmoded three years ahead of schedule.

With this increase in the number of passengers and new jets that carried more people would come increased costs.

"Nashville can expect to spend several million dollars in the next few years for construction of a parallel instrument runway, among other expenditures for terminal facilities," Tune said. A new runway was needed to speed landings and takeoffs, Tune believed. However, the landing of planes was just part of the problem. The new Boeing 747, which was scheduled for introduction the next year, was capable of carrying 500 passengers. It also had 10 passenger doors plus several others for cargo.

"The loading and unloading of passengers is a major problem with this type aircraft," explained Tune who also was a licensed commercial pilot and a lawyer.

In an article, he attributed Nashville's air traffic growth to "normal population expansion, cheaper fares and the city's geographic location in the jet stream used by planes going east and west and north and south."

"Another growth factor," Tune said, "is the city's dynamic economy."

At that time, the city was served by 12 major airlines.

"Each time a plane takes off or lands, the respective airline pays a fee based on the weight of the plane. It is with this fee and the leasing of space to the airlines that the city receives most of its revenue for operating an airport," Tune explained.

He argued that the proposed Airport Authority "would serve not only to take a burden from the taxpayers, but it would provide for the orderly movement of mounting air traffic in the future. It would issue revenue bonds and guarantee payment of them."

Tune predicted an Airport Authority "could easily save Nashville taxpayers $80 million plus interest during the next 10 years."

In the interview, he also explained how this new concept of governance would work. According to Tune, "if an Airport Authority were established in Nashville, it would purchase all airport properties from the city and end the system whereby the mayor appoints an aviation director and the council appropriates money for new construction or issues bonds to keep abreast of modern times." Under this system, he continued, this Airport Authority "could purchase the city's $3.1 million in airport properties and assume an $8.7 million bonded debt through a loan or loans."

Tune pointed out that "resolutions establishing the Authority, providing for its initial seven-member commission and an ordinance to transfer Metro property to the Authority, should be ready for introduction to the council soon."

He included this information because at the time of this 1969 interview, the Tennessee General Assembly had already passed enabling legislation to authorize municipalities to create airport authorities.

This enabling act, the Tennessean pointed out, stated that "before any action is taken by the council on an Airport Authority, a public hearing must be held on the question."

The act further stated that "…the governing body of the Authority shall be a board of commissioners of seven persons appointed by the executive officer of the creating municipality and approved by its governing body." Board members "shall have no financial interest in an airport or its concessions."

It also said that the commissioners "shall include a person of good standing and reputation in each of the following fields: engineering, law, industry or commerce, and finance."

The act also provided for appointing representatives from surrounding counties (such as Rutherford and Williamson) if these municipalities decided to participate in the Authority but limited this representation to no more than two members of the board.

Finally, the act declared that the commissioners "will be appointed for terms of seven years except the first group who will serve from one to seven years, depending on the order of their appointment."

And, of course, the legislation gave the council the power to remove any member of the board of commissioners by a two-thirds vote of the council.

In making his case for the adoption of this form of governance, John Tune again pointed out that Nashville's airport was nearing capacity. With the total number of plane movements presently at 275,000 annually and expected to increase to 880,000, Nashville's airport would also certainly reach its practical total capacity of about 400,000 in the next few years.

This "mushrooming of air traffic make the establishment of an Airport Authority essential," he argued.

Tune also stressed the importance of appointing the right people to the board.

A "group of weak-kneed commissioners" operating with a strong aviation director could cause problems," Tune said. "That is our greatest risk in an Authority," he said and added, "we will need – we must have competent and dedicated people."

Tune's arguments in the media and before groups around the county paid off. After this special enabling legislation was passed in 1969, Memphis formed the Memphis-Shelby County Airport Authority that year. A few months later, Nashville would join Memphis as the first two cities in Tennessee to adopt the Airport Authority structure (Knoxville formed its Airport Authority in 1978 and Chattanooga followed suit in 1985).

An Airport Authority with a Mission

Under the state statute adopted in 1969 by the Tennessee General Assembly, any city in Tennessee with a population of not less than 100,000 could form an Airport Authority which would have the essential powers of a self sufficient governmental entity.

"The structure of the Airport Authority was a genius concept," said Robert Mathews. "It gave the community the confidence it needed to pursue major aviation goals, and it gave the airlines, the FAA and bonding agencies the confidence to engage our region in a positive way that had not been possible in the past."

On Feb. 3, 1970, the Metropolitan Council of Nashville and Davidson County by a vote of 33 to six authorized the creation of the Metropolitan Nashville Airport Authority (MNAA) to operate as an independent enterprise – a self-sufficient public corporation.

Key elements of the proposal provided for the MNAA Board of Commissioners to be appointed by the mayor of Nashville and confirmed by Metro Council. The Authority would purchase and own the assets of the airport. Operations would be funded out of landing fees paid by airlines, from proceeds from concessions such as retail stores, advertising and parking and from leases with major tenants such as rental car companies.

Improvements and new infrastructure and facilities were to be financed through bonds underwritten by federal funds available to the nation's airports through the Airport and Airway Development Aid Program – renamed the Airport Improvement Program (AIP) in 1982 – and by the air carriers serving Nashville. Major air carriers entered into signatory agreements with the Authority, through which airport infrastructure would be underwritten, essentially guaranteeing a break-even operation for the airport. In turn, the airlines were granted oversight of the Authority's annual budget. Subsequently, the federal government in 1990 approved Passenger Facility Charges (PFC) to augment the AIP as a source of funds for airport infrastructure.

The Authority's Board of Commissioners would serve without pay and were to be responsible for setting guiding policies for the Authority. Each member was required by law to have expertise in a specific field deemed crucial for airport success. Those disciplines include law, finance, industry, commerce and engineering. At least two members must be FAA-certified pilots. (Originally calling for a seven-member panel, the act was amended later to increase board membership to 10 commissioners. Of the 10, at least one must be a female and one must be black. Representatives from surrounding neighborhoods were added in 1986 and the mayor of Nashville was added to the board in 1988.)

The board is responsible for hiring the president of the Authority to implement policy and manage a professional staff in the operation of Nashville International Airport and John C. Tune General Aviation Airport. Responsive to their roles of oversight, the board now has standing committees, which interface with the president and the managers of various departments.

The idea of having strong volunteers professionally designated for specific roles on the Authority was the lynch pin in attaching the economic engine of the Authority to other elements within the public and private sectors of the community.

Eddie Jones, who was then the CEO of the Chamber of Commerce, explained that John Tune structured the Authority to bring a level of excellence to specified areas of airport management. He wanted "to put together a group of people who had personal experience and knowledge of all the disciplines that you needed to run a business or an airport or any other successful organization."

Carolyn Tune echoed Jones' belief.

"I remember John telling me that it was critical to have the board organized so that it would not be subject to political influences which can change from one administration to the next," she recalled. "The professional and business qualifications were mandated so that the element of politics was reduced and to ensure that the people who served were really interested and knew about aviation and knew what needed to be done. John felt that was very important. John also felt the community needed people who could give the view of private aviation as well as public aviation."

John Tune's vision for a form of governance free of politics and run like a business had become reality with a mission to match.

The Metropolitan Nashville Airport Authority's primary functions were to own, plan, construct, operate and manage Nashville's airport system (along with Nashville Municipal Airport, this also included a general aviation airport). It was also to promote commerce and industry through air transportation. The Authority was to be a self-supporting, self-financing public agency to operate the airport without benefit of local tax dollars. It would be managed by the same economic standards used in private enterprise.

In March 1970, the Airport Authority issued bonds guaranteed by airlines landing fees and income from concessions and bought the airfield from the city. The airport was transferred to the Authority in exchange for 15-year payment of Metro government's cash equity, and retirement of all outstanding general obligation bond debt.

Since the inception of the Authority, no local property tax dollars have supported the operation of Nashville's airport. The Authority operates within a revenue budget that is balanced annually.

Two of the greatest benefits of the Authority structure were (1) it enabled the airport to be operated like a market-driven business and (2) it provided management continuity that enabled the Authority to begin long-range airport planning with the community, to serve Nashville's future.

Cultivating Additional Service Through a Unique Concept

The MNAA was launched prior to the deregulation of the airline industry in 1979. The routes flown and rates charged by air carriers were determined by the federal government. Airlines provided services on some routes that were marginally profitable and some that produced a loss in order to meet the government's objectives, which included providing service to many remote communities. There was no hub and spoke system in those days. There was intense competition as growing communities across the country sought additional air service.

One marketing approach taken was actually a continuation of efforts the Chamber of Commerce had initiated before the Airport Authority was established. This plan involved hosting two-day airline conferences to which the top management of airlines was invited. Organized by the Chamber of Commerce, the events were designed to give the airlines' decision-makers a profile of the economic and cultural excellence of the city, including opportunity for business travel and tourism. In the process, the visiting executives participated in insightful panel discussions on aviation and a series of presentations and events concerning Nashville and Middle Tennessee. As a result, the leadership of the community established lasting bonds with many of the airline executives who would chart the course of the deregulated industry during the coming years.

Robert Mathews, then a member of the Junior Chamber, recalled that one of his assignments was to provide transportation by car for airline VIPs. Many even stayed in private homes during their stay in the city.

"The Chamber realized that air service was the key, but to get air service, you had to be connected to and involved in the process," Mathews noted. At the time, he pointed out; the airlines didn't have total control over the routes they flew due to a regulated system. There were political pressures in those days, he added. Community leaders had to convince the airlines and the government to provide service or reroute service to their cities.

Later, with deregulation, the airlines could fly where they wanted and many of the relationships forged during the earlier airline conferences paid huge dividends in the form of air service to and from Nashville.

Carolyn Tune wasn't sure if the idea for the Chamber's airline conferences originated with John Tune but she knew "he was just vitally interested in them."

Her husband saw a great need to invite different presidents of the airlines to come to Nashville. "He was selling Nashville to them and in most instances it worked really well. He just thought that it would be a really important and fine thing for this city to have an increased amount of carriers coming in here," she added.

For example, she said her husband early on knew the president of Delta and "realized this man really had a vision for Delta. At the time Delta was a very small airline," she noted. "And it absolutely came to pass because Delta was built to be a huge airline. He felt like that was the really good thing about bringing these men in for these airline conferences because you got to know them and you got to understand what their vision was and if it coincided with yours and what they could do for Nashville."

Eddie Jones recalled that the Authority, initially operating in a regulated environment, almost immediately adopted the Chamber's concept of airline conferences. Jones described these airline conferences, held every other year, as "a two- or three-day dog and pony show and golf tournament and champagne dinners, all wrapped around the very serious business of negotiating new routes for our city and region. The idea was to convince them that this is the place they need to think about relative to their route structure."

Jones admitted it was "a strange invitation" and they had no idea how it would work out but they invited only the CEOs – no substitutes or designated representatives. He thinks they got just about every CEO they invited to the first one.

"They were regulated in those days, and while they were competing every day, there was less pressure and nothing to prevent the very top executives from coming together. That changed after deregulation, and one carrier or another dominated Nashville and other hub cities.

The Chamber and various businesses pitched in to help with the costs of the conferences. The airline executives were met at the airport with limousines, given the best rooms in town, treated to first-class entertainment and taken to the top of what was then the National Life Building for a black tie dinner and a look out over the city at night.

"It was pretty impressive," Jones remembered, but added, "It wasn't all just fun and games because we did extensive, in-depth research on the facts and benefits of this market, its potential, its directions and trends, where we saw growth. We were also prepared to discuss any shortcomings. And when they left they had an enormous amount of valid research on the city, and we knew it was in the right hands…the decision-makers. It hadn't been mailed to somebody who put it on the shelf. The right people got a good look at Nashville and carried with them a good projection of why Nashville was a good place to invest their assets and personnel, to beef up service."

Apparently no other cities were doing this, he believes, but it enabled members of the MNAA to get on a first-name basis with the senior officers of the airlines and create a whole new set of relationships that hadn't been there before.

The relationships cultivated with the airline executives during the airline conferences in Nashville also would be key to cultivating air service in later years. The airport's low landing fees as a function of good management also were an attraction for getting new service.

Second only to the issues of safety and efficiency, the MNAA made air service its ongoing priority to ensure that the airport would fulfill its role as a major economic engine in Nashville's future. It became obvious as deregulation loomed that renovating and expanding the existing terminal, runways and related passenger facilities would be the key to keeping the airport at the forefront of Nashville's future.

Extensive long-range planning was needed to make all this happen.

Operating in a Regulated Environment

Chapter 6

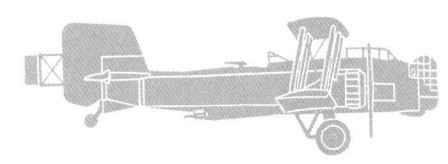

Chapter 6
Operating in a Regulated Environment

Building upon information and insights gained through their extensive contacts with airline executives and upon almost constant contact with elected officials and departments at the federal level, the leadership of the MNAA understood the impacts and the potential advantages of deregulation. And they began to prepare for it.

When the federal government returned the airport to the city in 1946 at war's end, the site had grown to 1,500 acres. By 1970, the airport's boundaries had extended to 2,800 acres. (By 1977, that number would increase to 3,300 acres, thanks to the foresightedness of Airport Authority board members such as Pat Wilson who pushed for the acquisition of more land for the airport.)

When the MNAA Board took over the airport in 1970, the facility now was served by nine airlines with 84 daily flights to 56 markets. That year Nashville's airport welcomed 1.3 million passengers and processed 25,329 tons of cargo.

The Airport Authority realized these figures would only increase and began planning for this future growth.

The long range planning of airports is mandated by the federal government and is based on FAA traffic projections for various regions of the country. Almost immediately after its inception, the MNAA responded like a market driven business in developing a comprehensive, 20-year long-range plan, which was completed in 1972. The issues were complex and there were diverse opinions within the community concerning the alternative solutions. One focus of discussion was the location of the airport to which visitors came and went via Murfreesboro Road.

To Move or Not to Move, That is the Question

Shortly after the Airport Authority was created, probably about 1971 or 1972, Robert Mathews recalled, the board sought the advice of consultants regarding the airport location. These consultants thought the "airport should be moved to an outlying area, away from the immediate downtown."

"Sky Harbor was an airport out near Murfreesboro," he noted. "I think they were recommending some land perhaps out toward there."

One suggested alternate location, Nelson Andrews remembered, was Cockrill Bend. "There was a small airport there (now site of the John Tune Airport). Another suggestion was to relocate in Smyrna, out in Rutherford County."

While he recalled the debate on the airport's location, Andrews doesn't remember any great political hue and cry to tear it down or any massive effort to put it some place else.

"I never thought there was any real chance that it was going to go to another place," he said. "It just made too much sense to keep it where it was, at a location that was close to the city and convenient to our interstate highway system and other major roads.

"That never got real far as far as I could see, although we spent a lot of time with the Rutherford County people," he said. "I thought it was destined to be where it is. I think, too, that not many people questioned John Tune's thoughts about it."

John Tune, along with Pat Wilson and other sitting board members overrode the consultants' advice to move the airport to some hinterland, Mathews reported.

"He was one who overrode the consultants," Carolyn Tune recalled, laughing. "Oh, I do remember that very, very well. They paid the consultants and they wanted to move the airport to Smyrna. I'm sure there are some people today who would say, 'I wish they had.' But John really felt it was a great location and Smyrna was a long way from downtown Nashville. He just felt like it would be better to remain where it was, and so they overrode the consultants. He was really committed to the fact that it needed to stay where it was. It's really wonderful to have an airport as centrally located as it is. When you think of how far in some cities you have to go to get to an airport. He just thought that (the current location) was best."

Eddie Jones too is aware of what the current location means to hospitality and tourism as well as to individual citizens. "When I have guests in town, and you probably do too, I can get my car downtown and, 10 minutes later, I'm at the airport. Visitors just can't believe it."

Jones remembers the thoughts of moving the airport to Smyrna. "As I recall, the conversation about that was of short duration. Everybody looked at how much land the airport had, what its future needs probably were and it went away about as quickly as it came up," he noted. Even after Dell moved in recently and took some of the land adjacent to the airport, "they've still got plenty of land out there."

That's because MNAA members like Pat Wilson, who was involved with discussions to relocate the airport, not only were opposed to it but in turn had pushed for the MNAA to acquire additional land at the current location.

While the relocation discussion pre-dated General William G. Moore's tenure, he too had to deal with this issue when the environmental impact study for a new runway was done in the late 1980s. Some of those opposed to the expansion raised the question of the airport's location, asking why it is in town and why it can't be out of town.

"They thought that there were a number of places where you could locate it," the General recalled. "We reviewed the study which had been done before my time and which was very good and which recommended that it be located here."

The reasons given in that previous study were then presented to those who would like to see the airport moved. The main reasons were costs, especially considering the infrastructure that would be required to put an airport where one doesn't already exist.

"When you go out and build a whole new airport and you build runways and duplicate runways that already exist, you're taking on enormous costs at a questionable increase in productivity and decrease in noise irritation," General Moore explained.

"When you look at the area we have here and compare it with other larger facilities, we've got over 4,000 acres here to work with. The big airport in Atlanta Hartsfield does not have quite 4,000 acres I've been told. (Hartsfield Atlanta International Airport covers 3,750 acres to be exact.) We have better expansion capability here than most any other airport of which I'm aware.

"Our businesses profit from having this airport close to the city," the General added. "When you can say that you're 10 minutes from the airport from downtown Nashville and then you start thinking of other cities that say, 'well, we're within an hour or within 30 minutes of our airport,' it makes quite a difference."

The MNAA obviously felt that way in the early 1970s as well. After looking at and evaluating six sites, they had resisted the consultants' advice to relocate the airport and proceeded with plans to expand at the current location.

General Moore thought this decision to leave the airport where it was – made before his time – was "absolutely the right decision."

Mathews agreed that one of the board's greatest decisions was to keep the airport at its present location. He also lauded the MNAA's long-range planning efforts.

Planning for the Next Two Decades

A 1973 Master Plan provided for expansion of the existing terminal, a new terminal and a new runway, to be triggered by demand. Forecasts indicated that all would occur before 1990. The area to the west of the airport was fully developed with residences, businesses and heavy industry and was not topographically suited for future terminal development. The plan called for expansion to the east to permit the construction of a new terminal, runway and taxiways across Donelson Pike.

Once the community and the FAA approved the 1973 Master Plan, the Authority gained airline commitment to the plan through a Statement of Intent signed by each of the major carriers serving Nashville at that time. The next step was to execute a long-term lease agreement with the carriers, to guarantee fiscal integrity of the airport.

In 1974, the MNAA issued its first airport revenue bonds. The bonds would be retired through the payment of airline and other tenant fees and charges. The Authority operated its business prudently and was able to keep all airline rates and charges highly competitive with other markets.

That same year, 1974, Southern Airways (now Northwest Airlines) had launched non-stop Detroit service. By the mid-1970s, the West Terminal, which had opened in 1961, was becoming congested and dated. Concourses were crowded.

In January 1976, plans were announced for a $5.1 million terminal renovation and expansion from 145,000 square feet to more than 180,000 square feet. That year also, the MNAA changed the airport's name from Nashville Municipal Airport to Nashville Metropolitan Airport.

The terminal renovation project was completed a year later. Chief among the changes was the addition of 12 "jetways" – enclosed bridges or ramps that enabled passengers to board or depart planes without going outside. Other features included three new aircraft gate positions, new ceilings, lighting, wall décor and carpeting; an expanded gift shop and a snack bar; enlarged concourses and departure lounges; and a baggage claim area expanded by about 50,000 feet and three more baggage carousels on the inside. Wider curbsides and traffic lanes and a covered walkway to the parking lot were added on the outside.

Nashvillians had a chance to view the improvements to the terminal at an open house at the airport on April 30. During the festivities, American Airlines demonstrated "computer ticketing" – a new way to assign seats and pay fares.

The day before the open house, the Tennessean reported that MNAA board member Jud Collins, a vice president with WSM Inc., while speaking to a group of visiting airline executives, thanked them for their support for the Nashville Airport. (Airlines had agreed in 1975 to pay higher landing fees to finance the airport terminal renovation.)

Collins also noted that when the 1964 Master Plan was developed, officials had predicted Nashville would see one million passengers by 1980, but the airport already had passed that mark in 1967. He predicted Nashville would soon pass the two million mark in passenger traffic. His prediction was right on target. The airport served 1.9 million air travelers in 1977. Once again the airport had outgrown its terminal facilities.

Deregulation Fosters Increased Growth for Nashville's Airport

The historic Airline Deregulation Act passed by Congress in 1978 went into effect the following year and with deregulation of the airline industry, the pace quickened at Nashville with new airlines and services. Updated passenger forecasts brought the old terminal capacity closer and triggered a master plan update and environmental assessment for the new terminal.

Robert Mathews observed the effect of deregulation both before and after he assumed his responsibilities on the MNAA Board.

"The Airport Authority and a knowledgeable leader – a president with a sophisticated staff – were able to react quickly in a positive way to make sure that the air industry was beneficial to Nashville. In other words, we didn't bureaucratize it to the point that they were waiting on us. The Airport Authority was ahead of the curve."

At the time, every city was competing for a hub and even the sophisticated people running the airlines weren't sure about the future, he recalled.

Mathews was sitting on the Board's Airline Affairs Committee that dealt with the airlines and negotiated contracts "and controlled your money.

"We were talking about this new terminal and talking about the size of it and what it ought to be. I remember this Delta person said, 'I don't care what you do but our vote is not going to allow you to build any more gates than you have leased to the airlines right now. We're not going to let you speculate on any future gates. You're going to build 25 and you're going to have them all leased before you break ground. And the second thing is, as soon as that terminal is finished, you're going to tear down that old terminal on the western side so that it can't be used like the airport Love Field (in Dallas).'"

Mathews added that other cities took a real gamble and they built 50 gates. Now, they're only using half of them, which is a burden to the taxpayers in those cities.

In 1980, MNAA enlarged the West Terminal to 188,000 square feet. Improvements included increasing the size of departure lounges and gate areas and the addition of loading bridges. These improvements were completed in the fall of 1980. At the time, the airport's land area had increased to 3,300 acres and the airport had three runways. That year, nine commercial carriers and four commuter airlines served the city. The airport, consequently, served 2.3 million passengers in 1980.

Without doubt, the city's aviation adventure was enjoying the fruits of deregulation.

In 1980, the Airport Authority revised the 1973 Airport Master Plan and began an environmental assessment for a new terminal on the northeast side of the field.

Meanwhile, because the new terminal would be on the other side of the airfield, the first construction projects were for taxiways to connect the existing airfield to the new terminal apron. These projects were eligible for 75 percent federal funding, but legislation for the Airport and Airway Development Act had expired at the time. The Authority borrowed $5 million and began construction in 1982. The Federal Airport Improvement Program was subsequently renewed in time for the airfield work to continue without interruption.

In 1983, MNAA broke ground and began construction for the John C. Tune general aviation reliever airport in the Cockrill Bend area of the city. Planning for this facility began in 1965 when the airport was still under the city's Department of Aviation. Officials realized the city needed a general aviation airport to better serve smaller privately owned aircraft, especially as jet service at the main airport expanded.

John Tune had pushed for a separate general aviation airport, according to his widow Carolyn Tune.

"That was something that he really wanted to happen and made happen," she said. "He really felt as the commercial airport grew, a general aviation airport managed by a fixed-base operator was an absolute necessity. Actually, his position was that the big companies should have to have their hangars at fixed base operations rather than at the airport."

After the MNAA was formed in 1970, the Authority set out to make this proposed general aviation airport a reality and conducted a site study in 1972.

The FAA approved the Cockrill Bend site and the Authority bought the property using a state grant. The chosen site was west of town and convenient for owners of private aircraft. The new reliever airport guaranteed capacity for continued growth of general aviation in the region. And this particular location would help relieve congestion at the main airport which was experiencing increased service from commercial aircraft.

During the 1970s, Nashville's airlines had grown from 10 to 13; passenger traffic increased by 77 percent to more than 2 million; daily flights more than doubled to nearly 200; and the number of markets served grew by 41 percent to more than 75 cities.

To assure capacity for continued air service growth, the Authority had expanded the north-south runway and reconstructed the airfield.

During this period, projects such as the Lockheed air cargo demonstration and the Nashville Airlines Executives Conference brought Nashville to the widespread attention of the national aviation industry. Such activity also captured the imagination of the community to see the limitless ways the airport could and would be a major key to Nashville's future.

To accomplish its ambitious goals, the MNAA put its trust in new leadership during this era of deregulation and growth. This leadership came in the form of one retired U.S. Air Force four-star general who was in sync with the Authority's vision.

New Leadership and Growth Under Deregulation

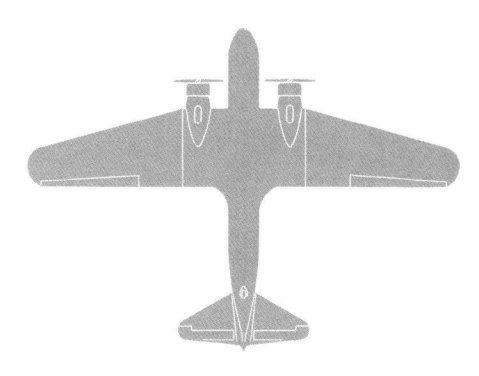

Chapter 7

Chapter 7
New Leadership and Growth Under Deregulation

As deregulation began to affect aviation in Nashville in the 1980s, members of the MNAA board sought to strengthen its management team to deal with the issues of aviation which were growing more complex.

The structure of the airline industry was being redefined. The role of the federal government in the regulation of domestic air service was diminished, but its involvement in air traffic control, safety and the construction of airports was never stronger. Federal funding for new facilities was constrained, as the Airport Improvement Fund became a tool in the balancing act to contain the nation's bulging deficit. Increased activism among neighborhood groups near airports resulted in growing demands to reduce aircraft noise and insulate nearby homes and businesses.

Technology was revolutionizing the capacity and capabilities of aircraft and reshaping the way in which airports were designed and operated. Many airport managers had been trained and came to professional maturity during the period in which the airline industry had been regulated. As a result, it was difficult for many of them to respond to the demands of change. The leadership of the MNAA Board of Commissioners was determined that its management team would be up to the task. In addition, the board also took an introspective look at the way in which it was operating.

"When I first got on the airport board, you got a sense that the president came up through the ranks. The board was still nurturing the system, the staff and really it had to be that way because, after all, they really were the creators of this idea, but they created it when the industry was regulated," Robert Mathews recalled.

After Mathews had been on the board a year or so, the then current president, Charles Griffith, died suddenly. Mathews, Tune, Franklin Jarman, Pat Wilson and Jack Dewitt formed a committee and sent out a request for candidates to apply.

"We hired this fellow who had a great resumé to come in to run the airport. He was just great on paper, but when you had a problem you couldn't find him. He was not a people person. We knew that he and the board were going to be better off by finding another person to serve as president," Mathews explained.

By now the board members had refocused their attention to establishing policy and were not quite as involved in day to day operations. But, without a strong president at the helm, they continued to be drawn into the details. Mathews recalled.

A chance meeting between Pat Wilson and General William G. Moore Jr. would provide an answer to these problems and open the doors to the next chapter in the city's aviation adventure.

The General Takes Command

A Texas native, General Moore began his military career in 1940 when he enlisted in the Army Air Corps as an aviation cadet. He graduated as a second lieutenant seven months before the Japanese attack on Pearl Harbor. Three wars and 240 combat missions later he retired from the U.S. Air Force in 1979 as a highly decorated and honored Four Star General.

During his career, General Moore had risen to the highest levels of military service and earned more than 40 awards and citations for valor and service. Just prior to retirement, he was commander in chief of the Military Airlift Command.

Not one to rest on his laurels, General Moore entered the private sector as president of Emery Air Freight, Inc. He subsequently provided consulting services to multi-national aviation corporations and served on the board of directors of several companies.

Then General Moore and his wife, Marjorie, moved to Tennessee. It was a decision based on experience. At one time, the general had served as commanding officer of Sewart Air Force Base in Smyrna.

Pat Wilson recalled his first meeting with the General.

"Marge and General Moore had decided that they wanted to live in Franklin after he retired. They had many cities they were looking at. I met General Moore at a cocktail party, maybe on a Wednesday, and was very much impressed with him. I asked if I could visit with him," Wilson said.

He recalls going once by himself to meet with the General. The next week, Robert Mathews, after being briefed by Wilson that General Moore might be the perfect candidate to direct the operations of the MNAA as president, joined them. The two commissioners met with General Moore on a Saturday morning and "we actually made him a proposition" recalled Wilson.

General Moore was busy with other things and said he would have to consider his current obligations, Wilson explained, but he showed great interest. "We felt good about the meeting," Wilson recalls.

General Moore, whose involvement with the MNAA prior to 1984 had been limited to being a passenger on flights in and out of Nashville, confirmed that meeting. Yes, Pat Wilson and Bobby Mathews had come to his Franklin home on Saturday and asked if he would consider assuming the presidency of the Airport Authority.

"We chatted for awhile generally about what the duties entailed. I realized that they were serious about the defined differences between the members of the board and the president. They correctly saw their role as one of policy. They saw the president's role, reporting to the board, as the implementation of board policy through effective management."

After telling Mathews and Wilson he would consider their offer, he had discussions with a number of the board members, "mainly because they wanted to know what they were getting. Those conversations worked out very well."

Former Mayor Richard Fulton recalled that General Moore met with him prior to giving the Authority his answer.

"I think we had lunch at what was then the Doubletree Hotel and Bob Mathews was the only other one there," Fulton remembered. "In addition to a number of very specific topics about the relationship between the city and the Airport Authority, General Moore wanted me to know that he was a Republican. He wanted me to know in advance, because he knew that I am a Democrat. Of course, he knew that. As mayor, you have to be nonpartisan in your approach, and I think that he'd say today that his political affiliation was never an issue between us. But I always had a good laugh out of him telling me he was a Republican."

When General Moore came to work in April 1984, his title was executive director of the MNAA. The title was changed to president later. He thinks the MNAA was the first in the country to use the title of president for its airport manager. "That was not the last thing that we changed through our initiatives," he said smiling.

When General Moore came in, "he took over. It happened in a matter of weeks. It became almost obvious overnight," Wilson recalled.

Introducing a Little Management to the System

The first really big job he had to do was to design more effective systems and get them developed and in place. And they had to change some attitudes and ultimately some people to make it work. He looked at a number of other airports that were "a little more mature in their development." He also brought on board a management consultant recommended very highly by other airports.

For two years, this consultant worked with the MNAA and spent a lot of time developing some of the necessary management systems, which are still in place in an improved form.

One example is the preventive maintenance program, which did not exist when he came on board. A piece of equipment was used until it broke down and then it was replaced without any effort to take care of it and make it last longer.

Consequently, preventive maintenance was one of the first things they worked on. Next came getting some planning going in maintenance so their workforce didn't have to wonder every day what was the best thing to do. Rather, they could come in daily with a purpose and an objective and with things to do. Also developed was a management information system, which incorporated all of the functions of management into a scheme that provided a coordinated and cooperative effort among maintenance people and all the departments in maintenance. These ranged from not only the preventive maintenance program but also inventory management, which included procurement control.

"We worked on management systems development for the first two or three years. It wasn't all we did but that was an important thing that had to get done because we could never operate this place the way it ought to be operated without it."

Developing a Mission Statement

In addition to putting management systems into place, General Moore directed the staff to develop a mission statement for the MNAA and the airport.

"After a great deal of discussion, we came out with a staff-developed mission statement that focused on safe, efficient operations, outstanding facilities, community and customer service and economic development," said Moore. "For many, customer service and economic development were unfamiliar concepts. They had been conditioned to believe that the airlines were our customers and that passenger service was solely the responsibility of the airlines."

The mission statement read:

Our mission is to plan, develop, manage and operate safe, efficient and attractive aviation facilities and to provide superior services for residents and economic interests in Middle Tennessee.

After the staff came up with the mission statement, General Moore presented it on their behalf to the Board of Commissioners. The board, in turn, reviewed it and then adopted it.

To ensure everybody understood what he was talking about, before he went to the board, General Moore came up with a three-word slogan to go with this mission statement. "After all of this is said and done" he told the board, "what it means is 'Be the Best.'"

Employees got buttons and other items with this slogan imprinted on them so they would understand that the hallmark of this new mission statement was customer service.

"I don't think there's any question but that the primary reason this airport is here is to serve the community with the best air transportation that we can develop. And that is really where our focus is and that's our priority," General Moore emphasized.

"But when a person comes out to this airport it ought to be a no hassle kind of experience – an experience they can enjoy," General Moore said.

That's why customer service is a top priority, he stressed, adding, "that's what we pay more attention to than anything else, and I think that we've been pretty successful in that."

There are airports today that haven't gotten that message, believes General Moore who prefers to present the airline as a partner in serving the customer. At the same time, he stressed that "you must treat your partner right and fairly. Give it what it needs. Do your part."

Building a Better Terminal

Perhaps the biggest test for General Moore's leadership abilities came soon after he joined the MNAA in 1984. This priority was to help orchestrate the creation of a new airport terminal at Nashville Metropolitan Airport on the northeast side of the field.

When Robert Mathews joined the MNAA Board, the Authority had already selected Reynolds, Smith and Hills, an architectural firm based in Jacksonville, Fla. The firm, Mathews explained, was really good at designing the airside of an airport (which is the operations, runways, lights and control tower from the gate out to the airfield) versus the landside (which is roadways, parking and facilities inside the terminal).

The Authority then decided it ought to pick a local architect in combination with these architects that knew a lot about airports. The local firm was Gresham, Smith and Partners.

"We kept asking the team, 'what's the terminal going to look like?' and they sat down with some of the board members and asked what ought to be in the design and we all spouted out these things. And they came up with these drawings," Mathews recalled.

He chuckled as he recalled a meeting at the City Club with the team trying to sell the committee on what the airport should look like. Pat Wilson made a charge to the architects on designing this new terminal.

"We had a design and I didn't like it," Wilson explained. "None of the others did either, but I was doing the talking. I said, 'you've got to use your talent to develop something else.' Well, the architect said, 'you tell me what you want,' to which I answered, 'I don't know what, but I'll know it when you produce it.'"

"Finally, we realized there was no way that the team could jointly come up with the design," Mathews continued. "We sat down then with the director. I guess John Tune said, 'why don't we just split them up? We're obligated to both of them. Let them come back to us with a presentation of what the terminal ought to look like.' Good idea. So I said, 'okay, we'll pay you off. Now you're separated.'"

The firms "started to squabble," Mathews added. The Jacksonville firm wanted someone familiar with Nashville and turned to Earl Swensson. Gresham Smith sought out a "design guru" out of New York.

His name was Robert Lamb Hart and his firm was the principal planner for Walt Disney World in Florida.

"Also, we had designed some buildings in Nashville," Bob Hart commented. They included the Northern Telecom national headquarters building and Nashville House at MetroCenter, which introduced a lot of new ideas into Nashville at the time they were designed. "They don't look all that revolutionary now but they were at the time,"

Hart explained, "and I think because of that the board had a lot of confidence in what we could do as part of a team with some local architects."

Although the firm had not designed any other airports, Hart thinks this helped in their selection. They offered a fresh approach.

"In fact that's what they were looking for, a fresh approach to airport design because they wanted to stand out, they wanted to be distinctive. And so the fresh approach was important to them," he said.

"The design committee that included Bill Weaver, Jack DeWitt and Pat Wilson, among others, listened to the presentations from the firms and finally decided upon one," Mathews added.

"And that's when Pat Wilson said, 'That's it. That's it.'" So after rejecting unsuccessful design attempts by others, the MNAA in mid-1984 charged local firm Gresham, Smith and Partners and lead design architect Robert Lamb Hart to design the terminal with that indescribable quality that was just right for Nashville. This was the first airport designed by either firm and became the launching pad for a major initiative by Gresham Smith in the design and engineering of airports in other cities around the nation.

The Story Behind the 'it' Design

Just what was the plan that won over the MNAA? Hart thinks that by "it," they wanted the building to be a Nashville landmark.

"It should be a fine public building. Great cities have a group of fine public buildings that sort of represent the community and express the character of the community. And I think that's what Pat Wilson and Bob Mathews were talking about."

There were other "intangibles," he added. In addition to this landmark idea, they were talking about "a place where we're going to be welcoming visitors to Nashville and the building should say, 'you've come to some place special. That this is a city that cares about itself. It is a sophisticated city. We're more than just business as usual here in Nashville.' And we had to capture that feeling. The Board wanted us to capture that feeling so when it appeared we had, that helped sell the concept to them.

"It had to be more than that, of course," he continued. "It had to be efficient and compact. In fact, we tried to make it seem more compact than it is. Let me put it another way. We wanted to make the point at which you enter the building as a distinct, very clear focal point. In fact, the whole thing is planned around the flow of people and making it clear, comfortable and also an exciting kind of experience out of your flow – the flow of people from the curb out to the gates. So we had to concentrate first on the functioning of the airport and that's where we worked with the airline committees and the engineers."

"We thought it was very important for the building inside to be light, open and airy and kind of an uplifting place. You feel good when you get there. And somehow it expresses a little bit of the excitement of travel and flight. At the same time it is a clean and comfortable kind of place," he noted.

On the outside, as one of the team members said during one of their presentations, "it looks like the green hills of Nashville."

"It really did. The green glass sort of mimics the rolling green hills in the back of the building. I can't say if we were trying to make it look like the green hills of Nashville but the fact that it did was very much in the spirit of what we were trying to accomplish," Hart said. "We wanted a building that felt like Nashville, that tried to capture some of the spirit or the look of Nashville."

The design firm proposed a pier finger configuration – a central terminal with two concourses with room to expand (in fact, two more were added later). They selected this layout for several reasons.

One was to make it easy for visitors to navigate. They would know where they were and where they were going if they could actually see where that was.

"We lined up the concourses with the main ticketing lobby in a way that once you were in the lobby you could see all the way out there. You could see clearly your destination," he explained. "It could be it was a long way away, but there was no confusion. There was no mystery about it."

"We felt that that was kind of a reassuring thing. You're not going to get lost here. You know for some people, travel involves a lot of anxiety, and so we were trying to make it so simple and clear that it wouldn't be confusing."

Another facet of designing a building like this is its durability, he explained. A public building gets very hard use from people carrying baggage and banging into things and the kind of heavy equipment used for cleaning to just the numbers of people. Durability to keep costs low and maintenance ease was an extremely important factor.

"You've seen durable public buildings that look industrial. To get durability at the same time we had this light, open airy feeling and this sort of high quality look were tough things to combine," Hart acknowledged.

The team most of all wanted this livelier, more spirited kind of place to be one that enhanced the passenger experience, something not many airports were doing at the time.

The MNAA obviously liked all the ideas presented and placed its confidence in Gresham Smith and Bob Hart.

"I think there was a feeling that we could bring a point of view and a level of sophistication to the design that would assure them of getting this landmark that they wanted, a building that would be uplifting and exciting and would say, 'hey Nashville's a pretty special place,'" Hart said.

In a few short months the architectural team produced their plans, and the new terminal design was unveiled in December 1984.

Plans initially called for a 27-gate, 400,000 square foot terminal to be completed by 1988. At that time, $128.5 million in airport revenue bonds were issued to fund its construction because terminals are not eligible for federal funding assistance. Timing was perfect because tax law changes on Jan. 1, 1985, would have substantially raised the cost to the airlines. This bond issue required the approval by a majority of the airlines. Approval was unanimous.

Site preparation began on the new terminal. But first, workers had to move Donelson Pike about 700 feet to the east. The road ran through what would become the parking lot. This was done at federal and state expense. While this was in progress, a new development occurred.

Back to the Drawing Tables to Include an American Hub

The need for a new and larger terminal was reinforced in June 1985 with American Airlines' announcement of its selection of Nashville as its major north/south regional hub.

When Nashville decided to build a new terminal, American had not told the MNAA the airline was going to put a hub in Music City. Until this time, Nashville didn't have the capability of handling the passengers associated with a hub. Now it would.

General Moore recalled the first time he heard of American's plans. He was in New York for a meeting with the bond underwriters. A representative from American was there with the Nashville group and suggested they ride out to the airport together. During this ride, he told the General that American was seriously considering putting a hub in Nashville. Since this was privileged information, General Moore couldn't talk about it. But, he was told, Nashville would hear from Robert Crandall, president and CEO of American, very soon. And they did.

American in their early discussions with General Moore, Robert Mathews and Pat Wilson talked about the need for Nashville to build a second north-south runway. One was scheduled for completion for 2000. American needed it in two years. The American representative also said the airline was considering building a maintenance base as well as a hub in Nashville. They planned to put up $25 million for the base but expected at least 20 percent as an incentive. He told the General, Mathews and Wilson that other cities were offering to provide funds as incentive to the airline to locate elsewhere.

"We decided we had 50 acres we could put in the package but that wasn't enough," Mathews recalled. They turned to Mayor Richard Fulton with this request for $5 million in the next two years. The mayor agreed to get the funds from the next year's budget.

"I told them they had it," Fulton remembered telling General Moore and Mathews, and he came up with the money. As it turns out, American backed off from the maintenance base.

"They didn't use it," Fulton confirmed. "I think we ended up using some of it for noise abatement when they built the new runway."

Later, Fulton was asked to go to Mexico City to an airport conference because "they wanted me to have lunch with the head of American Airlines at that time and they thought it would be good to have the mayor there. So we did meet with Mr. Crandall at lunch and shortly thereafter, there was an announcement made that Nashville would be the site of a hub," he remembered.

Crandall had already put his signature on building the terminal, the General recalled, but the airline needed something else. When an American senior vice president met at the University Club with the MNAA Board to finalize the agreement for their putting a hub in Nashville, he reminded them of a very important part of this agreement. He wanted to be sure the MNAA understood that American had to have a new runway and they had to have it by the end of 1989 to meet their expansion plans here.

"We had talked about that several times at the lower level," noted General Moore, "and we had said, 'yes, we can do that.' So American's guy turned to our Board and said, 'now General Moore has told us that you can have a runway operational by 1989. We want to know from the Board whether or not you agree with him.' Pat Wilson spoke up and said, 'you're damn right we do.'"

With that, Nashville's aviation adventure got "extremely interesting," the General mused. As soon as American publicly announced its plans for a new hub, the homeowners and some businesses located near the airport suddenly recognized that they were going to have the construction of a major infrastructure project in their neighborhood. In addition to dealing with the construction, the expanded airport was expected to create noise…and lots of it. In response, the MNAA began to develop under FAA guidelines a comprehensive plan to deal with neighborhood concerns about noise. The Authority also had to escalate work on the terminal to complete it by late 1987, a year earlier than planned. And it had to make good on its commitment to build a third $50 million runway by 1989, a very short time frame…and 11 years ahead of the schedule that had been projected in its 20-year plan. The combination of issues confronting the Authority would dominate its direction for the coming five years and add dramatic new chapters to the history of air service in the community.

Getting funding for a new terminal and a new runway and getting them completed within a set time frame so the American Airlines hub could open would have been no small task in itself. The MNAA had to accomplish this while dealing with a newly formed group for Nashvillians who opposed the planned improvement to the airport. Legal and financial constraints and federal bureaucracy threatened to delay or derail and possibly put an end to plans for the terminal and runway and jeopardize the American hub. How could the MNAA overcome these obstacles?

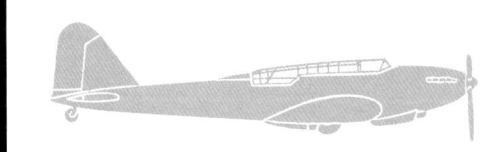

Overcoming the Obstacles

Chapter 8

Chapter 8
Overcoming the Obstacles

Challenges were nothing new to the MNAA. Funding was one of the first obstacles. According to the General, the first big break came around June 1986 with the Tax Adjustment Act of 1986, which allowed a provision of financing only to the end of the fiscal year.

"We had been trying and those who were here before I was were trying to get a new terminal built. We were living and working in an old decrepit, hard to manage terminal facility that was too small for the trade, the traffic," recalled General Moore.

"This act said that if we could get the financing prior to the end of the year, we could do it under certain conditions. We knew they were going to be floating a long-term bond in order to build this terminal. The conditions would result in a reduction in the long-term cost of the terminal by $40 million if we could meet them. So we set about trying to meet it. We got our experts in plus a New York underwriter outfit – people who at least understood what underwriting was and what we had to do – and we went to work.

"In the old terminal my office was in one spot and right next to it was a conference room. Every once in a while somebody would come in and say, 'well, you know, we've got a piece of this. I don't know if we can get this thing solved or not.' I just simply wouldn't take no for an answer. We had until midnight December 31."

Efforts went back and forth for months. Then, the day before the deadline, one of the underwriters on the bond issue pulled out.

"We were really floundering. And the guy we had in New York at that time just gave a marvelous job. I guess he screamed and hollered and kicked people in the rear end. And got our law firm activated and we got another underwriter to take the place of the fellow who pulled out," the General recalled, "with about 30 minutes to spare."

The last ditch effort completed just a half hour before the deadline was worth about $40 million over the terms of that bond issue and enabled the MNAA to finance the new terminal facility.

"More important than that, or as important, the General added, "it allowed us to go to the airlines with a very positive story then, and get their approval for building the terminal."

Until then, the airlines had approved only the initial stages – the foundation, the clearing and grading and site preparation. They had not approved the building of the terminal, he explained.

"We were able to go to them and say, 'you guys go with us and, if we can meet this deadline, it's going to be $40 million, which we and you are not going to have to put up.' And that was a pretty convincing story," General Moore observed.

While the MNAA was racing to meet this one deadline, another obstacle surfaced.

Mitigating Noisy Circumstances

In the spring of 1986, the Airport Authority had implemented a Noise Control Plan to mitigate the noise resulting from increased operations, deflecting it away from densely populated residential neighborhoods. This was the first step toward the development of a comprehensive noise mitigation program that was designed to achieve land use for the airport that was compatible with the surrounding areas. To expedite implementation of the noise control plan, the Authority extended its "preferential" nighttime runway, 13-31. MNAA also began its neighborhood assistance plan with a voluntary acquisition program in Airport Estates, a residential community located directly south of the airport across Murfreesboro Road.

The Tennessean on Aug. 30, 1987, recounted that a group of residents near the airport began to voice their concerns. They asserted that increased noise from the airport would reduce their property values and damage their quality of life. In October 1986, Neighbors Organized to Insure a Sound Environment (NOISE) filed a lawsuit in federal court to halt construction while an impact study was done, charging MNAA had failed to assess the cumulative impact of the terminal and proposed runway.

Meanwhile, the article continued, the Airport Authority issued an impact study that projected 160,000 people eventually would be seriously affected by noise. Costs of noise abatement were estimated as high as $100 million. In March 1987, MNAA committed $40 million for measures that included buying homes in areas most affected by the noise, soundproofing homes in other areas and noise "easements" for some homes to compensate for nuisance. The MNAA's Noise Mitigation Policy and Land Use Strategies Study was preliminary to the Part 150 Study that would address the majority of properties in the Authority's $95 million Neighborhood Assistance Program.

Two months later, in May, U.S. District Judge Thomas A. Wiseman dismissed the suit against MNAA, saying NOISE waited too long to file and that it failed to prove airport officials did not act within federal guidelines in assessing the airport's potential impact.

The MNAA didn't just rely on the courts. Rather, it adopted an aggressive community relations plan. General Moore attributes the success of this plan to the structure of the Airport Authority, which at that point was a seven-person board.

"Each commissioner had a role to play in the oversight of our operation. We asked commissioners to serve on one or more committees, which interfaced with the management of our departments. We must have had four or five committees, including a community relations committee, for example. We brought on board a first rate communications firm as consultants. With their help we put together a plan and we implemented it. That plan stimulated communications with the community, understanding what their concerns were and trying to deal with them and meeting with them frequently. It addressed the concerns of politicians who were obligated by virtue of their office to represent the people in the neighborhoods. It involved media relations and it utilized the very strong support we have with the business community, centered in the Chamber of Commerce. It was a demanding and assertive plan with specific goals, timetables and measurements. And that's what we did. We had some rancorous meetings. It was a little sporty at times and took an awful lot of time.

"The problem that we really had to deal with on noise mitigation at that time was it took so long," explained General Moore. "The financing was so tenuous that people mistrusted us. They didn't believe that we could do what we said we were going to do. And there were times, I must admit, that I wondered if we had extended ourselves too far.

"We set a goal and we publicized it that we were going to complete this noise mitigation program, which at that time was estimated to be $55 million in cost in five years. And to my knowledge, nobody had done that before."

The FAA provided 80 percent of the noise mitigation program, and the MNAA had to get them on board and supporting the program in order to meet the five-year goal. They enlisted the aid of Congressman Bob Clement.

Previously, if airports used local money for noise abatement before receiving federal funds, the federal government would not reimburse them.

"With the help of Congressman Clement, we were able to get a new law passed. He, as a first term Congressmen, did something almost unprecedented. He ran that legislation through the Congress and the Senate and got it passed. With that authority, we could fund the project with local funds and then be reimbursed by the FAA for its share later," General Moore added.

On Aug. 4, 1989, President George Bush signed the Noise Reimbursement Act, enabling the Airport Authority to proceed with its noise mitigation program. The legislation, sponsored by Congressman Clement with the full support of Tennessee's Washington delegation, had far-reaching airport industry benefit and was a critical issue for Nashville because of the substantial cost and essential timing of the MNAA's Noise Mitigation Program.

This voluntary program, begun in late 1989, was completed in 1995. It included acquisition, sales assistance and sound insulation involving more than 4,200 properties.

"Although the noise program expanded from $55 million to $90 million, it was still completed in the five-year time frame."

The Noise Reimbursement Act of 1989 did for the noise program what the Letter of Intent did for the funding of major construction projects at airports.

While wrestling with the Noise Mitigation efforts, General Moore also was guiding the construction of the new terminal and attempting to build and complete a new runway by the end of 1989 in order to acquire the planned American Airlines hub.

Design for the new runway was completed in 1986. That same year, construction of the new terminal progressed rapidly. The site was dedicated and the first concrete was poured in April 1986; the building was topped out in September of 1986.

Anticipating the increased air traffic that would accompany the American Airlines hub opening, MNAA opened its general aviation airport in 1986 to help relieve some of the congestion at Nashville Metropolitan Airport. The John C. Tune Airport opened with one storage hangar and 10 T-hangars.

Also in 1986, Berry Field quickly expanded its old terminal for an early "mini" hub opening in April.

In the midst of this bevy of activity, the MNAA was searching for funding and trying to fulfill the federal regulations required for building this new runway, a key to improving service, in record time.

The first obstacle came with the location selected for the runway. When the engineers brought the plan in, the site selected was just where MNAA wanted it, but it spanned a recently closed rock quarry. More importantly, the estimated completion date was a year too long.

The engineer went back to the drawing board and came back in with a new plan that stretched six months beyond the deadline. They were told, "it won't do. We are committed to having it completed by the end of 1989." So they brought a plan with the desired completion date, but when they presented the plan, they said, "we have to tell you, honestly, in our opinion, it's impossible. You can't do it." MNAA said, "well, thank you for the plan. We'll buy that one."

With plan in hand, the next step was to determine how to finance it in record time.

Like all airfield programs eligible for federal assistance, funding to construct the new runway was to be granted in increments prior to construction of each segment, over an extended period of time. This process made it impossible for the MNAA to meet the November 1989 completion deadline.

"The way the FAA financed projects at that time just made no sense at all," explained General Moore. "They would finance individual segments as separate projects. There was no continuity. It made no sense."

So the General went to Washington and talked to the FAA and told them, "We can't meet our deadline." After the first meeting, the MNAA attorney and General Moore weren't getting anywhere and the General asked, "Who can approve our program?"

They then took a different tact by getting Tennessee's Washington Congressional Delegation and the Director of the FAA personally involved.

"We went through four Congressional committees plus the FAA hierarchy and got adopted a device called the Letter of Intent."

The concept of this Letter of Intent, which was approved by the FAA in the spring of 1987, requires understanding how the Aviation Trust Fund works. This federal fund is collected from a percentage of ticket purchases for the purpose of improving the infrastructure of airports in the U.S. Airport authorities could apply for these funds to use for everything from land acquisition to infrastructure. Supposedly, once these airport authorities justified a project, they would receive a commitment that the funds would be paid as needed.

However, during the financial crisis in the U.S. when deficits were so high, those funds were always there but they were never allocated because they, along with some other funds, served as a balance to the deficit. So, these funds were slow in coming, but they were bankable. They were there. They were due the airport authorities, but weren't being released.

"Once the FAA had signed off their obligation in the Letter of Intent, then we could go to the financial community and they would support us. We could borrow the money," explained the General.

"Being able to visualize, design and implement an entire program start to finish, then walk up to the banker and get the money to do that entire program has got to be the least costly way," the General concluded.

That's why a Letter of Intent – which had never existed before – was so important. For the first time it allowed a project's sponsor to pull a big project together into one piece and finance it, and construction could proceed without interruption.

"When we had that, then we had what we needed to have a good, sensible construction program that could be managed and could be completed in a short space of time," he said.

With this commitment by the FAA to reimburse the Authority for the eligible federal amounts, according to their regular schedule, the MNAA was able to issue airport revenue bonds to cover the project.

Once again the MNAA was able to adapt itself to federal legislation and set a precedent that would revolutionize the aviation industry. The Letter of Intent program opened the door for a lot of airports and expanded so rapidly, the FAA had to put a cap on it.

Assessing the Situation Environmentally

Alas, the battle was not yet over. Another critical document the MNAA had to have was the Environmental Assessment.

"The rules are pretty strict on Environmental Assessments. The estimate for our project was two years. We couldn't stand two years. We had to get it in less than a year. We called a meeting in Atlanta with the FAA, the environmental people and the airport people and we kicked it around," General Moore said.

The MNAA then pointed out to this group that the longest piece of that environmental assessment, as far as approval was concerned, was in the FAA. It had to go from Nashville to Memphis. Memphis had to send it to Atlanta. Atlanta had to send it to Washington. And then it came all the way back down again. And that was what was taking all the time.

"We suggested, 'why don't we do it at Nashville?' They thought about that and said, 'you know, that's not a bad idea. We need to change our system anyway.' So we worked out a deal with the FAA to eliminate Memphis – with Memphis' agreement," the General said. The environmental assessment would go straight from Nashville to Atlanta, Atlanta to Washington, and then back from Washington to Atlanta and Nashville.

"Not only that, but they provided the man who had the approval authority over it in Washington. He came to Nashville, and we set up a word processor in our conference room and together we wrote the document, which he was going to approve. And which he did," recalled the General.

The MNAA had obtained the new runway Environmental Impact Statement (EIS) fast track approval in October 1986. A year later to the month, the EIS for the new runway was completed. The FAA, in turn, approved the EIS a month later in November 1987. Clearing for the runway began immediately.

A New Airport Terminal and Runway for Nashville

Chapter 9

Chapter 9
A New Airport Terminal and Runway for Nashville

Planning for this new runway, to be completed in 2000 as stipulated in the 1973 Master Plan, had begun at the same time site preparation was nearing completion for Nashville Metropolitan Airport's new terminal, set for completion in 1988. The terminal had already been funded and site preparation was well under way when the MNAA successfully negotiated the selection of Nashville for the American Airlines hub in 1985. However, because the hub came along while the terminal was in the design stage, there was still room for some flexibility to incorporate American's needs into the design, according to architect Robert Hart. The Authority agreed to accelerate the construction schedule for completion in 1987 and to increase the size of the new terminal from 400,000 square feet to 750,000 square feet.

Consequently, the terminal was designed as an American Airlines hub, Hart confirmed, but the design team also incorporated the needs of other airlines as well as the MNAA staff.

"Once the team was selected, our firm was involved in every aspect of the design, gathering information, all the operating requirements, working closely with the staff. Also, we had several meetings with the airline committee, a committee comprised of the planning officials from each of the participating airlines, and they established a lot of the criteria for the building," he recalled.

The MNAA had already assembled some projections for the growth of the airport and the number of gates that were needed before his firm was involved.

Hart noted that the Airport Authority had a very good project manager who ran this on behalf of the Airport Authority and he gathered all the information that was needed.

As the terminal construction neared completion, the MNAA began making plans for a grand opening event. Unfortunately, it had no way to fund such an event.

Robert Mathews recalled, "the plans for the new airport terminal were great, and the building probably turned out better than the plans. It was very impressive," he noted. "So we decided we were going to have some kind of a grand opening. We were struggling about how to do it. We wanted to have all these people come out."

MNAA called on Opryland's E.W. "Bud" Wendell to ask for his help.

Wendell does remember their meeting well.

"I think it's amusing now. General Moore and Bobby Mathews came to see me when they were opening the new airport," he explained. "Just the two of them. They had called and wanted an appointment but didn't tell me what they wanted. They got in my office and they said, 'We have this problem and we need your help.' I said, 'well, what's the problem?' They said, 'we're going to open this new airport (terminal) on such and such a day and we want to really do a big community event, but we don't have any money.'

"I think that was just a sign of a good working, cooperative relationship because I thought it was important too that they open that airport terminal with a bang and a lot of benefit and awareness for the community. So I said, 'yeah, we'll do it. We'll open it. We'll just take it off your hands. Forget about it.' And we did."

Wendell said he delegated responsibility for the event to Jack Vaughn, who was accustomed to developing major events for major national meetings and conventions at Opryland Hotel.

"Bud Wendell deserves all the credit," Vaughn insisted. "He just told me what to do and I did it. All in all, it was a tremendous, tremendous gala at the airport. It was just magnificent. But Bud really is the one who put it together."

Unfortunately, Wendell ended up getting pneumonia and didn't attend the opening. "They told me it was spectacular," he remembers.

The Dream Takes Wing

On Aug. 30, 1987, less than a year after the building was topped out, the new $104 million, 750,000 square foot terminal opened, following a series of new terminal events for various groups throughout the region. (Counting taxiways and parking, the price tag read $200 million.)

With much fanfare, the "Festival of Flight" dedication ceremonies on Sunday included high school marching bands, tours of the terminal and free concessions. Tennessee Governor Ned McWherter, Nashville Mayor Richard Fulton and MNAA Chairman Robert Mathews cut a huge decorative ribbon wrapped around the speaker's platform. The huge decorative ribbon symbolized that this was a gift to the citizens in a 100-mile radius.

"Nashville's new airport represents 'the vision Tennesseans have for the 21st century,'" Governor Ned McWherter said during the ceremony, the Tennessean reported the next day.

The ribbon cutting and grand opening event featured country music stars, including Larry, Steve and Rudy – The Gatlin Brothers and Lee Greenwood, who entertained the estimated 20,000 Nashville residents who came to dine on free hotdogs and other refreshments and help celebrate as "the dream took wing."

Mathews still remembered Lee Greenwood singing "God Bless the USA." The Chamber of Commerce got involved," he added, "we had 800 invited guests at the opening. We tried to make sure nobody was left out. It was a big deal and great fanfare for the city.

"If it hadn't been for this relationship with Opryland and the other community leaders who realized the significance of the aviation system, the event wouldn't have happened," Mathews believed. "It was really a community event."

Among those attending the festivities, in addition to the public and state and local dignitaries, were many of those responsible for making the dream happen. An insert in Sunday's Tennessean (Aug. 30, 1987) gave a history of the airport and listed those responsible for the new facility. They included:

    Gresham, Smith & Partners – Gary Hunt, GS's managing partner

    Robert Lamb Hart – Architects & Planners, the architect of record for the terminal and concourse project (He also developed the master plan for MetroCenter in Nashville.)

Other members of the design team included:

    Burns & McDonnell – Aviation Architects & Engineers, Kansas City, Mo.

    Standley D. Lindsey & Associates – Structural Engineers, Nashville

    Williams, Russell & Johnson – Engineers & Architects, Nashville

    Thompson Consultants International – Facility Design Consultants, Los Angeles

    Hanscomb Associates – Cost Estimating, Cambridge, Mass.

    Barge, Waggoner, Sumner & Cannon – Engineers & Planners, Nashville

    Talbert-Cox – Airport Engineers, Nashville

The Tennessean reported on Aug. 30 that the day before the grand opening festivities, more than 6,000 senior citizens got a sneak preview of the new facility with its 46 gates as the Senior Citizen Orchestra performed. Airport officials were expecting only 3,000.

Robert Hart attended the opening events and the one thing that struck him "was how good the airport looked when it was full of people.

"We designed it to be full of people and all the time during the construction it was what construction looks like. And when we walked in and there were thousands of people in this wonderful, big space, the ticketing space, I found that a really fulfilling moment because that was the vision…of the people in this space," he recalled. "It was a pretty good party they put on too."

Hart was also pleased with the feeling the building gave off once it was completed, which is one of those intangibles the MNAA was striving to achieve.

"Architecture is an idea, a language, it speaks too. You can't avoid it. Once a building is built, there the message is. Approaching the building that way was something that the Board felt comfortable with," he explained.

"Buildings can give you this sort of excitement and an uplifting feeling," he continued. "Architecture says things about the people who build it and it sends messages. And it also can express an attitude toward the people who work in the building and the people who are using the building. You know, 'we really care about you.' And when I saw the building full of people, it really gave me that feeling that we had accomplished that."

Another facet of the building, he explained, is that it "in effect orchestrates the movements, like the great railroad stations of the past. You walk in there and you know where to go. The building gives you clues as to where to go and we use a lot of lights and skylights to do that. And when you're in there, it dramatizes your movement. It makes you feel like you're doing something important when you're there too."

And their efforts paid off. After the terminal was built, American Airlines Chairman Robert Crandall made a point to tell Hart at one time that this was the best operating airport in their system.

"I also heard from some third parties who dealt with American Airlines that the operating people were thrilled with the airport. I think that that team effort made it easier to sell because it was truly a very functional, efficient, compact airport.

"Again, part of the function of architecture is to make it an easy place to operate and also to make it a pleasant place to work," Hart concluded.

Work began at the new airport in earnest when service from the facility began Sept. 14, 1987, 10 months ahead of the original schedule and within budget. It began serving seven million passengers annually.

In addition to American Airlines, major national airlines serving Nashville at the time included Delta, Eastern, Northwest, Pan Am, Piedmont, TWA, United, USAir and Southwest. Smaller regional (commuter) airlines providing service to and from Nashville included Allegheny Commuter, American Eagle, Comair and Florida Express.

Adding a New Runway to the Mix

With the terminal open, the MNAA could turn its attention to the new parallel runway (2R-20L). The new terminal had been in operation only for a couple of months when the construction equipment began moving brush for the new runway.

Three months later in February 1988, runway construction began. However, before workers could pour concrete for a new runway, they had to relocate Donelson Pike and fill a portion of a 25-year-old limestone quarry. This required moving 4.8 million cubic yards of rock and dirt to fill part of the quarry and blasting rock from the northeast corner and placing it along the opposite wall. A taxiway bridging Donelson Pike was built to connect the new runway to the terminal apron.

This new runway was constructed in less than two years – also ahead of schedule and on budget. In September 1989 to celebrate its completion, a series of public events saluted the history of transportation, ranging from a foot race, a bicycle race, and an antique car show to an aircraft display on the runway. The new 8,000-foot runway was dedicated and opened for service on Nov. 10, 1989.

The Tennessean on Nov. 10, 1989, reported Tennessee Senator James Sasser spoke to industry officials at a dinner marking the completion of the $78.5 million runway. At this dinner, during the biannual meeting of the Nashville Airline Executives Conference, Sasser called Nashville International Airport "a showcase for the nation." He noted that between 1980-1988, operating capacity jumped more than 300 percent to 3.5 million passengers and 18 million tons of freight.

"The FAA projects by 2005, Nashville will be among the world's largest and most efficient airports, moving 9 million passengers and 61 million tons of cargo annually," he added.

The article also noted 600 local, state and federal officials, including the FAA's Assistant Administrator Robert L. Donahue had breakfast on the runway that day. The Spirit of Nashville, an American Airlines 757 model, was the first commercial airplane to land on the new runway. Passengers aboard included American's President and Chairman Robert L. Crandall. The 200-seat jetliner made a low, quiet pass over those gathered for the event before landing. The 757 plane "was so quiet you couldn't even hear the thing land," Mathews recalled. According to the Tennessean (Nov. 11, 1989), Governor Ned McWherter declared the runway open following a rendition by a U.S. Army Band.

Also in late 1989, the MNAA completed a new, technologically advanced aircraft rescue and fire fighting facility, designed by its own fully certified, dual function fire fighting and police forces.

The airport's Department of Public Safety, which is housed there, provides police, aircraft fire rescue and emergency medical services to airport visitors. Its personnel are dual trained as police officers and fire fighters. In subsequent years, the department has grown to include staff to cover every thing from traffic enforcement to hazardous materials control. (The Airport Containment Team (ACT) was formed in 1994 to handle extraordinary crisis situations. That year the airport also formed what is now known as the Crisis Negotiation Team (CNT). Included in this area are special teams, including the Hazardous Devices Team, the K9 Bomb Detection Team and the Special Operations/Haz-Mat/Go-Team.)

After months of study to determine the best use of the old terminal, it was demolished in 1990. With facilities in place to handle growth, the MNAA undertook the task of diversifying services in an era of deregulation and growth.

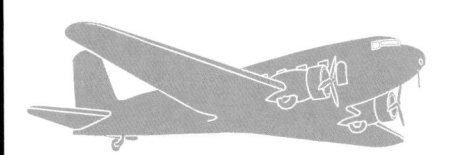

Diversified Services in a Deregulated Economy

Chapter 10

Chapter 10
Diversified services in a Deregulated Economy

Nashville Metropolitan Airport was poised to take advantage of new opportunities in a deregulated economy now that it had the facilities to handle this growth. Part of that growth included international service. The MNAA turned its attention to acquiring international flights while maintaining the level of service it already enjoyed.

Robert Mathews recalled that when the Authority was financing the terminal building in the 1980s, he was concerned about how they could keep a good bond rating and get a guarantee of these bonds with the airlines. Braniff had suspended operations in May 1988 and Eastern Airlines would cease operations in January 1991. And now airlines could fly wherever they wanted, thanks to deregulation.

"One of these advisers said, 'Don't worry about it because Nashville is in such a good location, it will always be served by airlines because you've got a very good market, so you'll always have a good rating.' And so that was a security blanket that I just adopted in my mind that we had such a great future," Mathews noted. His question was, "How do you play it the best that you can to the outside world?"

Eddie Jones also was aware of deregulation and the changes involved.

"I remember some anxieties that if an airline was not required to run a flight in here and it wasn't the best flight they had, that we were going to lose a lot of service. I guess the Airport Authority went in high gear trying not only to preserve and protect the level of service that we had, but really to grow it, which I think it did. As I recall, some other cities, Knoxville, Louisville, Chattanooga all drastically dropped down to just two or three flights a day or a very minimal level of service as the airlines bailed out," he added.

But those cities didn't have the relationships Nashville had with the airlines, Jones pointed out. Thanks to the city's unique Airline Conferences, the airlines' senior executives knew the city, knew the market and knew the commitment of the city's leadership and the commitment of the Airport Authority.

"All those things, you can't even put a price tag on them, they're so valuable," he added.

These relationships soon paid off with increased service to Canada.

In July 1988, the MNAA Board of Commissioners had voted unanimously to change the airport's name from Nashville Metropolitan Airport to Nashville International Airport, in preparation for the start of the first nonstop service to Toronto, which began in October 1988. A new airport entrance sign with the airport's new name was dedicated in 1990. In his 1991 presentation, Robert Mathews wrote, "A major goal of the Authority is to gain international service between Nashville and Europe, as well as additional Canadian flights."

That year, the Airport Authority's focus turned full scale to developing international air service and completing the infrastructure required to support it. This was a complex issue involving bilateral agreements between the United States and other governments. The Authority mounted an aggressive campaign to gain service.

The MNAA prepared the airfield with a number of improvements that occurred from 1991 to 1994. These included extending runway 13-31 to 9,200 feet in 1991 and further extending it to 11,000 feet by June 1993 to accommodate full overseas flights year round and relocation and extension of the center runway (2C-20C) to 8,000 feet by 1994 to accommodate future air service growth. The airport also built a new concourse in 1993 to connect existing concourses A and B, thus eliminating the need for connecting passengers to re-enter the security checkpoint.

When a window for London service emerged in 1993, the MNAA, having laid all of the groundwork, moved quickly with its Washington air service consultant to pursue it. Nashville was awarded the service – a nonstop American Airlines Nashville-London Gatwick route – in late 1993. Service was scheduled to start in May of 1994. Within 90 days of the award, the Authority had completed this new International Arrivals Building, bringing the passenger terminal to its present 820,000 square feet.

Nonstop London service began May 29, 1994, and continued for just over 15 months. American broke all records for cargo on the Boeing 767 aircraft and carried passenger loads averaging more than 70 percent and as high as 80-90 percent during many months.

In addition to the London flight and its regular domestic flights, American Airlines had American Eagle as a regional airline to serve the Nashville hub with about 140 flights a day.

"We were pleased by all this action," Robert Mathews recalled. "People were coming in from towns that had never been served by airlines."

One development that probably impacted American's change in plans was the fact that Eastern went out of business in 1991, leaving Miami wide open. American began moving aircraft from Nashville to Miami, downsizing the hub here in 1995. The airline eliminated Nashville's London flight in October 1995 and by September 1996 had eliminated its hub in Music City.

Even though the hub was leaving, demand for services remained high. In 1996 alone, Columbia/HCA booked more than 42,000 flights leaving from or arriving in Nashville.

Losing the hub simply meant finding additional service elsewhere to serve the general public and corporate clients.

"I believe in the management of alternatives," General Moore said. "When something happens that looks like a disaster, look at the alternative and then manage your way into it and through it and make something out of it.

"That's not something I've made up," he declared. "It's something I've watched happen here."

Southwest Expands in the Nashville Market

With the loss of the American Airlines hub, some in the community thought this would have a tremendous effect on the area. Although losing the hub meant fewer destinations, many of those would be picked up by other carriers.

One carrier that quickly filled the void was Southwest Airlines. Southwest had quietly entered the Nashville market back in March 1986, utilizing a refurbished former cargo facility adjacent to the old west terminal, rather than waiting for the new terminal's completion.

"I'm not sure how many people are aware that probably the day after the announcement of the American Airlines hub for Nashville, I had an appointment with Mr. Kelleher, head of Southwest Airlines," former Mayor Dick Fulton revealed. "He had called and wanted to come in. The appointment was at 4 o'clock in the afternoon and when he came in the mayor's office, he told me that he started to cancel the appointment because he was coming over to talk about the possibility of Southwest Airlines making Nashville a north/south hub. But since American was making it a hub, he didn't feel like it was the proper time to do so."

Fulton encouraged Kelleher to continue to serve Nashville even if he couldn't expand service at the time. So did Robert Mathews, who had a similar experience with Southwest's co-founder, president and chief executive officer.

"The airport operated very businesslike, very efficiently. We had very competitive landing fees. We were a place where an airline could come and make money," Mathews felt. Then, he recalled, just two months after cutting the ribbon for Southwest to begin operating out of the old terminal, American Airlines announced it was going to make Nashville a hub.

"Well, Herb Kelleher is a very, very smart business person," Mathews pointed out. When he asked Southwest's chief why he didn't stay in Nashville and "really load it up with flights" Kelleher told Mathews, "I'm not going to get in the same boxing ring with Joe Louis."

Mathews later reminded Kelleher of his comment, and in a move to keep Nashville at the forefront of the airline executive's thoughts, he arranged to send Kelleher a pair of boxing gloves, which still hang in his office today. "I wanted him to know that we expected him to stay in the ring for Nashville," Mathews remembered. "And he did just that."

When American went out, Kelleher came back in. At a subsequent meeting Mathews, Moore and other representatives from Nashville were in Dallas to present their latest plans for expansion to Southwest. Kelleher walked into the meeting and the first thing he did was to shadowbox around the room with Mathews. "But he never got in the ring with Joe Louis," Mathews added.

The interesting thing about all this is the MNAA could never have gotten the support of the FAA for funding (which came through the ticket tax) to build the terminal if not for the influx of flights from American, Mathews believes. "We could never have gotten the infrastructure." The American hub helped build the new facilities and resulted in national prominence for Nashville International Airport, he stressed.

While American helped provide the infrastructure, Southwest knew people and that airline's entrance into the Nashville market in 1986 turned out to be an important air service development for the city. Southwest had helped fill the void left by the departure of American's hub and helped sustain Nashville as a national aviation center.

"They've been a blessing. They really have," Eddie Jones agreed. "We really needed them when the American hub didn't work. That would have left an awful hole if Southwest hadn't jumped right in and grabbed up some of those vacant routes and in a sense added on," Jones said.

"My wife and I like to go to New England, and we have never been able to get into New Hampshire without going around the world and now we've got a direct flight from Nashville to Manchester."

Enter the O and D Passengers

"It was demoralizing to have a big promotion and pump the hub and celebrate this great victory and then see it shut down," Jones admitted. "But," he added, "I think they were off base on the hub concept. Not whether it was in Nashville or someplace else. You're still going to do some hub operations. I mean, Delta is in Atlanta, and TWA is in St. Louis.

I don't really know how much they bring to a city because they're basically transfer points. They're people who come in and jump off at Gate 18 and run down and jump back on at Gate 6. So what does that really do for you?"

Jones, in effect, had pinpointed the upside of this hub loss in Nashville. With the hub, the majority of the passengers in Nashville were connecting. They didn't go into town. They remained only in the airport long enough to go from one gate to another.

Without the hub, the city has experienced a major shift in the types of passengers in the Nashville market. Since 1995 when American Airlines began phasing out its hub, the number of travelers who begin or end their trip in Nashville – a segment of the passenger population referred to as O and D (origination and destination) – has grown dramatically and become the dominating factor in the airport's passenger mix.

Contributing to this increase are several factors: The mix of air service has changed, resulting in very competitive fares, and Middle Tennessee's healthy economy means more people from the region can afford to fly.

Since 1994, O and D traffic has grown by 48.6 percent. These travelers live in this region or are visitors who have Nashville as their destination. They spend more time in the Nashville Airport terminal as well as go into town for business and personal reasons.

"We're talking about regionalism," asserted Robert Mathews. "Nashville has finally come to the realization that it's a region and the Nashville Airport is the core of the region."

Now that Nashville has an O and D operation, connecting passengers have become the minority. With low fares now available, Nashville is attracting passengers from as far as Knoxville, Chattanooga and Jackson, Tennessee; Huntsville and Montgomery, Alabama; and Louisville, Kentucky, who drive here to get on an aircraft.

"Economically, it makes so much more sense," Nelson Andrews explained. "I fly Southwest a lot. I fly them so much, my wife can ride free any time I go. You see people all the time from Huntsville, from Kentucky, from Chattanooga, who come here. They drive a couple of hours here to fly Southwest because it costs a fortune if they're flying out of their own place. So probably the thing we've done best from a regional standpoint is the airport."

To further attract these flyers from other cities, the MNAA had to continue to offer quality air service from additional airlines. Even before the hub's closing in 1996 and American's downsizing it the year before, the MNAA had pro-actively launched an aggressive air service marketing campaign in early 1995. Its goals were to attract new carriers, increase frequencies and to add new nonstop routes. Since September 1995, Nashville has gained seven new airlines: Continental, Air Canada, Delta Express, United Express, Corporate Airlines, Skyway and Air Midwest, which is operated by USAir Express. While 11 airlines served the city in 1992, that number had grown to 19 at its peak in 2001.

All have had strong market acceptance. In 1998, Nashville saw its passenger growth on the airport's major airlines increase 4.6 percent compared with a national average of 1.3 percent. If charters and commuters are included, passenger traffic on all Nashville's airlines was up 5.2 percent.

To accommodate this increase in O and D traffic, the Nashville Airport undertook several improvements, including the addition of a satellite automobile parking lot. In June 1998, the MNAA initiated a $35 million terminal landside expansion program. This program, completed in the spring of 2000, mainly affected the short-term parking garage, the facade of the terminal and the bridges and roadways. The short-term parking garage tripled in size to offer 1,700 short-term parking spaces. Bridges on the arrival and departure levels were 57 feet wider. More traffic lanes were added on all levels and designated for either private or commercial vehicles and shuttle and limousine loading. The first level of the terminal was enlarged for ground transportation services.

New features included covered pedestrian bridges, two new escalators and larger elevators and 140-foot moving sidewalks on the second and third levels in the short-term parking garage. Also added was a short-term baggage loading area; valet parking at curbside; four climate-controlled waiting rooms on the ground transportation level; and space for rental cars just outside the terminal building.

It was business as usual during the construction, which was spearheaded by Hardaway Construction Corp., and the project was completed on time and within budget. The MNAA enlisted the help of Robert Hart's firm on all of these additions and on the new parking garage.

"On all of those, we've stayed as design consultant to the local architects. We were the design architects working with the local firm Gobbell Hayes Partners. This combination again of a local architect and our firm was a way we've sort of kept the spirit of the place and kept the continuation of the ideas that everybody liked so much," said Hart.

Serving the General Aviation Community

In addition to the commercial aviation services offered at Nashville International Airport, the MNAA also sought to further enhance services for regional corporate and business leaders and individuals who owned their own aircraft.

"General aviation was a large part of our travel," explained General Moore. "There are few companies of any size which don't have airplanes to fly their staffs around. That generally is because they want to move fast, they want to move into cities that don't have good air service. They have businesses there."

He noted that businesses can cut costs over flying commercially by using their own planes properly – they can control the trips, who goes on the airplane and what kind of loads they carry.

"So it becomes a very desirable thing for business," he added.

"And then on top of that, you've got the private individual who loves airplanes, loves aviation. The aircraft may be a little 'one seater' or the owner may have a pretty good size airplane and needs a place to operate," General Moore continued.

Currently, the MNAA has responsibility for providing facilities for general aviation at both Nashville International and the 399-acre John C. Tune Airport which opened on July 20, 1986.

General Moore noted that "aviation is really blossoming because of the location of Tune and also because the air traffic is not as heavy over there as it is at the Nashville Airport."

Nashville's major corporations have contributed to this increased growth in general aviation with companies such as HCA, Genesco, Ingram, and Gaylord Entertainment frequently utilizing the services of John C. Tune Airport.

To meet increased demand for services, John C. Tune Airport has been expanded. A 3,600-square-foot modern terminal building opened in October 1995. The facility features a spacious lobby, a pilot's lounge, a conference room, a break room and a flight planning room equipped with computer access to weather services.

When this airport opened, it had one storage hangar and 10 T-hangars. Today it has two large storage hangars and 105 T-hangars. The approximately 360,000 square feet of aircraft parking and apron space can accommodate 69 tie-down aircraft. An Instrument Landing System (ILS) and Glide Slope for guidance during adverse weather and low visibility was installed in August 1999.

"We have a responsibility having the airport and providing facilities for general aviation. And that generally is in terms of the real estate we can devote to it and the kind of leases we can work out with the general aviation operators. We didn't build their hangars in this airport anyway. They had to build their hangars. But we made it as attractive to them as we could without losing money ourselves," General Moore explained.

The MNAA continues to provide for general aviation at both Nashville International and John Tune, so these smaller aircraft operators can land both places. But the more attractive and sophisticated John Tune Airport has become in terms of instrument landing systems and other services, the more use it gets and the more it has become a reliever airport, which means it takes some of the pressure away from Nashville International.

Cargo Service Takes a Big Step Forward

In addition to meeting the needs of general aviation operators in the region, the MNAA now offers a restructured cargo operation as another service of Nashville International.

"Cargo that is available on short notice eliminates the need for a large inventory in the warehouse of an assembly plant. As everyone now knows, that type of service has a direct impact on the bottom line of a company. They do not have to pay the interest on borrowed money to maintain a large inventory and the size of their warehouse can be dramatically reduced. So, as air service has become more and more adept at moving cargo quickly and protecting it while it's being moved, and reacting to short notice requirements, more and more of the cargo is moving by air," the General explained.

"With that comes an additional responsibility for an airport and that is to provide at least the facilities to support the best air cargo service that we can just like the best air service that we can provide this city. That gets pretty high on our priority list, particularly if you don't have the facilities."

The cargo facility at the Nashville Airport for years had been a private company facility, which, although started with good intentions and carried on with good intentions for awhile, began to deteriorate badly.

As recently as 2000, if anyone mentioned air cargo in Nashville, the response was to laugh and ask, "What air cargo?"

There was some service here offered by very good cargo carriers. But it was not nearly at the level or volume that it should be. Consequently, people were shipping cargo by ground or surface means to Atlanta, New York and Chicago when they could just as easily have flown it right out of Nashville. And because once the shipper has found a reliable method of transport and these systems are in place to serve them, they can't or won't just change these systems overnight. They're reluctant to change what works.

In addition to overcoming the effects of this rather long-term dissatisfaction with this airport's air cargo service, Nashville was hampered by a lack of air cargo facilities.

Furthermore, the need for improved air cargo service was spurred on by the American Airlines hub when it was here. American carried as much air cargo as could be put on the airplane in the 767 aircraft it was flying from Nashville to London. Several of those area companies in the business of shipping and forwarding cargo became used to having this kind of cargo service. When the American Airlines hub went away, they were just left floundering, General Moore recalled.

"An air cargo operator has to have channels to move goods and move it when it needs to be moved. We are not there yet in cargo services, but we are well on the way to dramatic improvement. We recognized that we would have to fill the gap just as rapidly as we could."

As soon as resources became available, the airport bought out the lease from the private company, took over air cargo and exerted a "fast, energetic effort," as he described it, to provide better facilities.

"At this point, we do have better facilities. We've spent some $6.6 million so far to double the aircraft parking apron (three to six aircraft) and we're getting ready to spend more to improve the air cargo. The air cargo traffic is now increasing, and we're better able to provide the kind of service that our businesses need in air cargo."

The Nashville Air Cargo Link complex, which is separate from passenger facilities, is located off Vultee Boulevard on the west side of the airport. This Air Cargo Link now serves local, national and international companies involved in shipping air cargo to and from the Middle Tennessee region. It also is home to air cargo integrators, charter cargo airliners and air express companies. Services to domestic and foreign markets include same-day shipping, charter, overnight cargo and customers brokerage.

The MNAA has set aside additional real estate now and has developed a plan for long-range air cargo development that could cover 143 acres.

Additional expansion activities in 2002 and 2003 have resulted in parking apron restoration and expansion to accommodate six B747-400 cargo aircraft and 49,000 square feet of additional air cargo terminal space. The addition of this space has already resulted in the addition of six times weekly international air cargo service provided by China Airlines to/from the Pacific region and Asia.

"With that, air cargo will be up to the level of service that it ought to be for a community with as much industry as we have, as large as this community is and still growing," the General said.

By putting all these diversified services in place, the MNAA was making good on its commitment to maximize the airport's benefits to the community. At the same time, the Authority, in keeping with its mission, was developing aviation's role as a catalyst for Nashville commerce and economic development.

Reaping the Benefits of Quality Air Service

Chapter 11

Chapter 11
Reaping the Benefits of Quality Air Service

Just as every airport and airline is part of a national and international system of air service, domestic and foreign passengers and businesses also depend upon a fully integrated multi-modal system of ground transportation incorporating first-rate roads, rails and water. Since the 1940s, Nashville's centralized location has resulted in the full development of every mode of transportation, and they work together to provide unusual opportunities for Tennessee's capital city.

While the MNAA was courting the airlines to acquire additional service, leaders in the community were anxious to convince the world that Nashville was a great place to do business – a great place to live and to work – a great place simply to visit and to play.

The goal was to have companies located or relocated here and for organizations to host meetings here or for tourists to spend their vacations here.

To accomplish these goals, the Chamber of Commerce and the MNAA formed a natural alliance. After all, quality air service had a direct impact on business development as well as the convention and tourism industries in Nashville and Middle Tennessee.

During the 1990s, more than 320 companies relocated to or started in the Nashville area. And the city in 2003 ranked among the Top 10 U.S. tourism and convention destinations.

Business Development Hinges on Air Service

"The top reason may be different from one company to the next, but air service is among those top three reasons why a company locates in Nashville," noted Tom Seigenthaler, head of a public relations firm which was doing work for MNAA. "It may be one, two or three, depending on the company, but it's virtually always in the top three."

General Moore agreed, "We have a couple of industries that would not be here if we had no airport in the first place and second place if we had no ability to provide their cargo needs."

Nelson Andrews added that companies look to the airport's capacity and future plans when making decisions to locate or expand in Nashville.

"From July 1994 until July 1998, 134 corporations relocated to Middle Tennessee," he stated, adding, "The MNAA works with the economic development departments of the state and Metro governments, with the tourism industry and with Partnership 2000."

"Partnership 2000 (later named Partnership 2010) was our effort to really put much more emphasis on economic development directly," explained Andrews, who was vice chairman of that endeavor.

"The airport is obviously a natural partnership with the Chamber. You cannot sell a move by a fairly large corporation into this area without having a first-class airport. It just can't be done. No way," Andrews stated. "And there's no way we would have attracted any of these big companies that have come in here if we hadn't had a good airport. Dell wouldn't have come in here if we'd had a rinky-dink airport. Couldn't."

Dell Computer had announced on Aug. 27, 1999, that the company would build a new manufacturing facility in Nashville. The Dell Campus, located adjacent to Nashville International Airport, opened for business in September 2000.

The partnership between the airport and the Chamber isn't new to the city, Eddie Jones recalled. While he was at the Chamber, they started a program similar to Partnership 2010.

"We called it Nashville Plus. It was a fundraising device to try to get more money into the Chamber to buy some national advertising. We wanted to get into the Wall Street Journal and Fortune and Business Week and to staff up the Chamber in its economic development area. And I think Partnership 2000 is sort of that same role, only bigger and better," he explained.

"Once they got the funding through Nashville Plus, they were then able to focus on Nashville's growing air service," Jones went on to say. "At that time we had plans for the old terminal. So between the Chamber type programs that promote economic growth, you always invest some funds in your air service, the Airport Authority. That's definitely because of the importance of air service on economic development," he agreed.

"One of the biggest economic development deals that I was involved in was Nissan," Jones volunteered. "They were going to build a manufacturing plant here but the Nissan major presence in the United States is on the West Coast in terms of management and distribution and whatever. They don't build anything out there. There was a good deal of study and consideration of 'Can we get our people from around the country and dealers plus our headquarters in and out of Nashville on an airplane?'"

Nissan announced plans to build its plant in the U.S. in April 1980 and five months later announced Smyrna, Tennessee, was the site. Ground was broken on Feb. 3, 1981, and the automobile manufacturer went into production in June 1983.

Jones also believes Saturn considered how to get back and forth to Detroit in making the decision to build a plant in Middle Tennessee as well.

General Motors announced plans to break ground for its new Saturn plant on July 30, 1985, and cars began rolling off the assembly line in 1991.

"Almost any prospect that the Chamber or the state was working with for relocation or opening up a new activity here, you had to spend a good deal of time convincing people that you had good air service," Jones explained.

"It's a factor in any big corporate decision," he said.

Selling the community to the airlines is a constant process for the Airport Authority. It involves comprehensive analysis of the community's needs, the capacity, capabilities and profit objectives of the airlines and an accurate assessment of the numbers of passengers that would be available on a desired route. Typically, presentations would be made several times each year by the Authority to decision-makers at various airlines. A team of individuals would go out to visit the airlines to show them gaps in service, which if filled, would be mutually beneficial to the airlines and to Nashville.

"Partnership 2000 and the Authority have been a team in working to attract additional air service," General Moore explained. "Working with the Chamber we have developed and shared information to determine the new service and additional frequencies desired by our community. We have given our financial support to Partnership 2000 and they in turn have provided funds for specific research and presentations and related marketing activities.

"Increased tourism is a by-product of aviation's growth and accessibility," he added.

"If people learned they could spend two or three hours of a vacation in an airplane getting to their destination as opposed to a day or a day and a half of that vacation time driving on the road, they liked it better," General Moore reasoned.

Pat Wilson agreed that having a good airport and good air service is a factor in promoting tourism. And Southwest with its affordable fares also has helped. American's London flight also exposed Nashville to an international market, Jack Vaughn noted.

"Even though the flight itself didn't last, just like anything else, it exposed Nashville to a brand spanking new market. The folks in London at that point in time were saying, 'OK, we're going to San Francisco or Los Angeles or to New York or New Jersey or what-have-you.' And all of a sudden here's Nashville, Tennessee, right in the heart of the Southeast. We showed them what we had to offer and I think over the course of the years, this has been very, very beneficial to Nashville," Vaughn said. He also credits Partnership 2000 with helping build the convention business in the city.

Good Air Service Also Impacts Convention Business

Closely related to tourism is the convention market, which is "one of the big growth factors still in this city," Eddie Jones agreed. "The convention planner, he or she is going to look at two things, air service and room rates. And most convention planners or the chief executives of national organizations (who really make the final decisions) make their recommendations to a board. But they're not going to recommend a city to their board where their members are not going to be able to easily access and egress by air or roads or whatever and where they won't get a good buy at a competitive rate on facilities and hotel rooms. So it's a big-time thing," Jones said.

"I think MNAA has been very mindful of the importance of the airport to building the tourism business, the convention business," E.W. Wendell pointed out. "We at Gaylord (Entertainment) would never have built the hotel that we did if we weren't comfortable with the air service because in the convention business, 50 percent of your attendees fly in. And so we worked very closely in creating the convention business. There was comparatively little convention business in Nashville until we built the Opryland Hotel."

Joining Wendell in this endeavor to jumpstart Nashville's convention business was one of his vice presidents, Jack Vaughn. Vaughn spearheaded construction and expansion of the 2,884-room Opryland Hotel and Convention Center complete with its two giant indoor gardens under glass. (It's now called the Gaylord Opryland Resort and Convention Center.)

Vaughn agreed with Wendell that air service entered into decisions about building and then subsequently expanding the hotel.

"We would never have built Phase II, Phase III or Phase IV without what the General created. It was just as simple as that. We had to have the transportation. We had to have the freight capabilities, and he made that possible by expanding the airport," he declared.

The cooperation from the airport made feasible the booking of unbelievably large conventions for which every city in the entire United States was vying. By having its own transportation system, the Opryland Hotel made it easy for groups to come into the City of Nashville and get on just one shuttle going right to its convention center. This in turn meant "we'd just pull more conventions, and more conventions meant more money and more vitality for the City of Nashville," according to Vaughn.

The cooperation extended to allowing the Opryland Hotel to locate a welcome center at the airport.

"Needless to say now, we paid for it. They didn't give us anything free by any stretch of the imagination," Vaughn added, laughing.

Freight is another aspect of the convention business that is dependent on the airlines.

"Freight is extremely expensive for major conventions coming in," Vaughn explained, adding, "The Opryland Hotel now has 300,000 square feet of exhibit space. There's no question about it as far as a major convention is concerned. Freight is very, very important – you know – getting those monster exhibits into the city."

He credits Southwest and Herb Kelleher with recent growth.

"I think he as an individual was instrumental. I remember that he spoke to the Chamber a couple of times. I recall his visiting with us. I think it was at the opening of one of the auto plants. He was very dynamic, very positive and very easy to be with. Herb Kelleher believed in Nashville and that has certainly brought us a long way now, as far as Southwest is concerned. He had several national promotions focused on Nashville when Southwest initially came in. We felt the positive impact of his work at Opryland, and I am confident that others involved in tourism locally did, too. So Mr. Kelleher was responsible for a lot of the success of the airport," Vaughn concluded.

"Nashville now is considered as one of the major convention cities throughout the United States. It's as simple as that, whether Southwest is a hub or American is a hub or what-have-you. You can get into Nashville, Tennessee, and you can get out of Nashville, Tennessee, without flying to four different airports before you get there," he added.

Wendell said that working with airline CEOs and having those friendships and relationships is something Nashville has done that other cities didn't do.

Another individual who cultivated these business relationships was Phil Bredesen, Nashville's mayor from 1991-1999.

Bredesen moved to Nashville in 1975 when his wife, Andrea Conte, went to work for HCA, and he carved out his own niche in the booming health care industry, starting and investing in several successful companies, including Healthplans, which later became HealthAmerica, and the Coventry Corporation.

As mayor he also spearheaded the construction of a $170 million 17,000-seat arena downtown, which contributed to the rebirth of lower Broadway and Second Avenue as a tourist destination.

Mayor Bredesen also negotiated to bring health giant Columbia/HCA's headquarters back to Nashville from Louisville, Kentucky.

Although the mayor took pride in his $330 million school upgrade and his $75 million library improvement projects, he will most likely be remembered for his efforts to bring professional sports to Music City.

Professional Sports Fly Into Nashville

Gaylord Entertainment and the Chamber also were big proponents for bringing professional sports to Nashville. Again, first-rate air service was a factor in attracting these professional teams.

The National Football League's Houston Oilers relocated to Nashville in 1996 and changed the team's name to the Tennessee Titans in 1999 when they moved into their new home, the 65,000-seat Nashville Coliseum. During the 1998-1999 season the National Hockey League's Nashville Predators took to the ice at Gaylord Entertainment Center.

Richard Fulton, who still serves on the Chamber's sports committee, knows the history of pro sports in Nashville.

"In my final year as mayor we made a bid for the Olympics. Fortunately, we didn't receive the bid," he added, laughing. "We came in third out of 12 cities that were vying for it. We didn't even have a football stadium. We didn't have the facilities. Of course, we could have built them. But it did generate so much enthusiasm that as a result of that, the Chamber created a sports committee to pursue professional sports.

"Obviously, that's been very successful," he pointed out. "We have the Music City Bowl Game, we have the Titans here and the Predators. It's been a great asset.

"I'm in full agreement," Fulton explained. "That's one of the advantages of having professional sports. Every time our football team is mentioned in the New York Times or USA Today or the Los Angeles Times, people think of Nashville. When that Goodyear blimp goes over the Coliseum, people all over the country and in other parts of the world see Nashville."

Fulton believes that a good airport and air service helped entice sports teams to locate here and make the investment. He added that the city would not have acquired the professional teams "if we had not had the good airport that we have and the airlines."

E.W. Wendell agrees, "We would have never gotten them if we hadn't had comprehensive air service. We'd have never gotten them. I don't think Bud Adams, owner of the Titans, would have even considered coming to a town that didn't have good air service and a well-run facility. It's just one of those building blocks that is necessary to have. I think Bud Adams would tell you that. He would not be here with the Titans."

"Your whole community is made up of a lot of different things," Nelson Andrews said. He mentioned the need to have reasonable educational, criminal justice and medical systems as well as a reasonable airport system. The strength of the Chamber and the strength of venture capital in a community are also things that are very important.

A city lacking in any one of these is in trouble, he feels.

The fact that other than New York City, Nashville has more colleges and universities than any place in the country, that it's a capital city or that a lot of people work in state government are all factors to look at.

Add to that all the city's attractions: the Frist Center for the Visual Arts, Second Avenue, the Country Music Hall of Fame, Cheekwood Botanical Gardens, Fisk University's art collection, the Grand Ole Opry, the Gaylord Opryland Resort and Convention Center, Gaylord Entertainment Center and Nashville Coliseum and all the city's sports teams. In combination, they are a major force in the city, a reflection of business and culture and a magnet for regional and national tourism.

One theory expressed is that while all these attractions could be considered show horses, or play horses for the community, the MNAA is equal to and possibly superior to all of them because it's the workhorse of the community. It does a job that no other entity does.

"It's a wonderful parallel. There's no question about it. It gets the job done for us, and we run out front and we take all the credit," Jack Vaughn agreed.

"The Airport Authority is in a sense responsible for their marketing, of being able to bring their constituencies into the Hall of Fame or the museum or a football game or whatever. I think the MNAA and the facility that it operates provide marketing support for our destination points," Eddie Jones reasoned.

Dick Fulton added, "I'd just say that it's part of the team of horses that have pushed Nashville forward."

Not to be overlooked is the MNAA's impact on the city's wealth of businesses – ranging from health care, religious book publishing, book distribution, recording and music publishing of all genres of music, finance and insurance to manufacturing of goods such as barges, shoes, aircraft parts, automobiles and computers.

Certainly, the MNAA's decision not to relocate the airport has been a factor in fostering economic development, especially with the business, tourism and convention industries.

"Nashville is truly fortunate to have the location of the airport where it is, so close. It's not 35 or 40 miles out from the city, which in many other cities is the case. We've got an ideal location. We're just 15 minutes from downtown," Jones added.

Wendell echoed that. "That's something we tend to forget until you get in a cab to go out to Dulles or somewhere else."

Visitors to the city are less than 15 minutes from the Gaylord Opryland Resort and Convention Center. Vaughn called the decision not to relocate the airport years ago "one of the most marvelous decisions they could have made.

"You arrive in any major city and you're a good hour away wherever you're going from the airport. In our case, you're a half-hour," he noted. "It is just magnificent. In just 10-15 minutes you're at your destination." And that's important to conventioneers coming in, he added.

The presence of these conventioneers in the community is just one benefit of quality air service. Having a great airport not only has helped with the growth and development of the business community and the tourism industries, but its operations also had direct impact on the local and regional economy.

Putting a Dollar Figure on the Airport and Air Services

In every respect, Nashville International Airport is a powerful engine that fuels the city's economic progress. It connects the city to the commerce and cultures of the world. It carries people to and from the city for business and pleasure on the almost 400 flights that depart and arrive daily.

The 19 carriers serving Berry Field Nashville (BNA) in 2001 provided nonstop or single-plane service to 87 cities in the U.S., Canada and Mexico.

Early in 2000, the MNAA commissioned a study on "The Economic Role of Nashville International Airport."

This analysis found that from 1994 to 1999, origin and destination traffic at Nashville International increased from 4.6 million passengers to 6.8 million – a 48.6 percent increase. The airport's growth in O and D passengers served exceeded that of Tennessee's other three major commercial airports (Memphis, Knoxville and Chattanooga) combined.

Unlike a hub operation in which passengers land, wait at the airport for a time and then depart on another aircraft, O and D passengers, on the other hand, either live in the community or have come here on business, on vacation or to a meeting or convention. Each of them makes a significant economic contribution to the city, and those who live here are generally involved in making it a better place to live and work.

In 1999 alone, the airport handled 8.5 million passengers and generated $47 million in revenues. Cargo shipments moving through the airport totaled 62,500 tons in 1999.

The airport served a trade area of 79 counties in Middle Tennessee, southern Kentucky and northern Alabama with a population of nearly three million people, all of whom live within a 100-mile radius of the airport.

Visitors to Nashville (3.2 million who come by air) spent approximately $2.1 billion annually for items such as lodging, meals, entertainment, other retail and ground transportation.

The study further found that the airport and the 3.2 million visitors had an impact on 56,611 jobs – that's a direct impact on 6,591 jobs and an indirect impact on 50,020 other jobs. The airport, air carriers and vendors servicing the facility employed 4,494 people and had a payroll of $143 million in 1999.

The multiplier impact created by the purchase of goods and services by the airport and airport-related businesses and the spending of wages by airport employees contributed to the regional economy as well.

As a result, in 1999, the airport had a role in providing $4.9 billion worth of commerce to Nashville and Davidson County's economy - $1.3 billion in wages and $3.6 billion in sales.

The study concluded: "A growing, active, well-operated airport is also important to Nashville and Middle Tennessee citizens and businesses because it greatly enhances the ability to attract new businesses and expand existing businesses. The economic development arena is highly competitive, and having Nashville International Airport as a well-managed, friendly, capacity-available facility is a significant advantage."

This economic study was intended to quantify and describe Nashville International Airport's current impact on the economy of the region. It also served to reiterate the future importance of continued development of the airport and its customer base "to benefit the businesses, individuals and future economic development of Nashville and Middle Tennessee."

Aviation certainly would continue to play a major role in the region's future development.

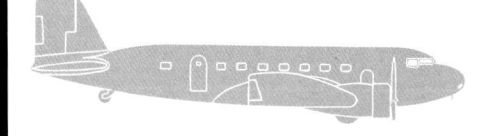

The Future of Aviation in Nashville

Chapter 12

Chapter 12
The Future of Aviation in Nashville

The future of Nashville's aviation adventure is clearly rooted in its past and its present. "Since 1937, Nashville's airport has expanded to meet air transportation demands that foster economic growth for Nashville and Middle Tennessee. Nashville once depended on barges and boats on the Cumberland for economic growth. Then it depended on railroads. Today, it is dominated by air transportation. The airport is certainly the 'lasting and useful improvement' Colonel Berry wanted it to be and as Mayor Hilary Howse probably envisioned it in 1935," Robert Mathews concluded in his 1991 talk before the Coffee House Club.

"Since 1937," he continued, "the airport has grown from its original 337 acres to over 4,000 acres. Its runway lengths have doubled and another runway added. It has become the crossroads of the nation. As Mr. Burr Cullom, special guest speaker at its dedication in 1937, said, 'it is an airport second to none.'" Fortunately, it has remained so compared to other cities of Nashville's size during the ensuing decades.

Former Mayor Richard Fulton agreed with this assessment and with the decision to acquire additional land and improve the airport facilities.

"Fortunately the Airport Authority and the airport's management have acquired additional land over the years," he stated, adding, "I don't have any basis for this, but I would think that facility has enough land for continued expansion for years to come."

Fulton added, "I think flying in and out of Nashville Airport is a joy when you compare it to flying in and out of some of the more crowded airports." He cited Dallas, Atlanta and New York as cities "where when you get off of the plane, you might have to walk a mile or two to finally get your bag and get a taxi and to get out. And if you happen to be changing planes there, you really have a problem.

"We're just so fortunate that the planning for the development of the Nashville Airport has been done by those that were looking to the future as far as expansion is concerned and the number of flights coming in and out. I just don't know how we could have any better facility."

The Airport Authority also has positioned itself to expand by acquiring property over the years from time to time, Eddie Jones noted.

"The airport has control of enough land to reach far into the future. This was very wise because the price of land goes up by the hour when owners find out the airport needs it," he continued.

"In addition, our terminal is good for some good long while yet. They may have to put another wing for additional gates, but I think we have a terminal building that will serve us pretty well into the future," Jones concluded.

The current terminal was designed with the capability of expanding up to a total of 60 gates. And when the present facilities reach capacity, plans for another concourse and another runway are part of the MNAA's design for the future of Nashville International Airport.

Nashville's 30-Year Aviation Plan Takes Wing

One of the most important things completed by the MNAA during the 1990s was the development of Nashville's 30-year Aviation Plan. Begun in 1991 and completed in 1993, it was intended to be the blueprint for the airport's future, and one of the keys to Nashville's future, just as the 1973 master plan was. This reaches out 10 years further than required, and it incorporates the collective thinking of this community and region.

The FAA requires all airports to have a 20-year master plan based on forecasts about the growth of the aviation industry. This long-range plan focuses on the interests not only of the airport, but also the general community, the federal government and the airlines. Such a plan enables the airport board and the community to look at future facility needs. It also alerts the FAA, which will finance or approve the use of PFCs for future infrastructure.

Once a plan is in place, all can look at what's being considered and if necessary make amendments to the plan or explain it.

In the fall of 1991, the Airport Authority started drafting a new long-range master plan. The board looked at information provided by the FAA, outside consultants and the airlines. The board members contributed their own creative imagination to the process. They talked about what lies ahead in the next five, 10, 20 and even 30 years for the Nashville Airport. Based on the FAA and airlines' projections on the number of passengers in Nashville, they asked what all this means in terms of a terminal and of an efficient operation such as a new runway.

"So we actually have a fifth runway planned 30 years out from 1991," Mathews noted. "No one knows if it will be built, but at least it's on the drawing board and it's going to be considered."

The long-range plan underwent community review and input from February through April 1993.

Another area of growth in the future is in cargo service. Nashville International completed the first phase of the cargo terminal's expansion in the summer of 2000. This $6.6 million project upgraded the taxiway and apron, doubling the amount of space used to park planes outside the cargo terminal.

On April 26, 2001, the Tennessean reported that the FAA had approved a grant of more than $4 million that will help expand the area used to service jets in the airport's cargo terminal. This second phase of the cargo terminal's expansion will allow the airport to better serve several wide-bodied cargo jets at the same time.

The article also reported the airport's Air Cargo Link reached a milestone the previous weekend when two wide-bodied Atlas Air freighter jets unloaded 156,000 pounds of cargo bound for Irish Express Cargo in Nashville. The jets also refueled here.

On Aug. 19, 2001, China Airlines began direct air cargo service from Taiwan to Nashville with four weekly 747-400 freighter flights. This international cargo service has since increased to six flights per week and is expected to continue to grow over the near term.

"With Dell and with other companies that are in a hurry to get a package out air cargo has to be a real and viable factor. And I think that our ability to service cargo will determine whether or not we are in the mix," Eddie Jones noted.

The emphasis on cargo service and facilities was among the critical issues with which General Moore dealt prior to departing the airport in 2001. He also pointed out and began planning on two other major issues with which future airport managers will contend. One is the environment. The other is the available capacity of regional airports like Nashville in contrast to the lack of capacity at major hubs such as Chicago, Dallas, Miami and New York. And, following the terrorist attacks on the World Trade Center in New York on Sep. 11, 2001 and subsequent apparent acts of biological assaults on U.S. businesses, he would add a third issue: responding to the need to provide safe, efficient air transportation in the United States in the future, in which new dangers could develop at a moment's notice.

Creating an Environmentally Friendly Airport

"Environmental concerns are involved in a broad range of issues and will have different impacts on varying sizes of airports," General Moore said. "Many characterize noise as a disruptive and harmful form of pollution and see it as the most significant issue. For others, the possible run-off of spilled gasoline, glycol-deicing fluid and oil are a primary concern. Some will cite the need to protect the natural habitat. Others fear that the concentrated use of airport facilities by automobiles creates a definite and definable problem. The truth is that they are all very important issues and each of them has found its way into public policies relative to the environment. They require an enormous amount of time in terms of planning and management, and remedial measures can be very expensive. And the impacts increase in direct proportion to the size and complexity of the airport and its operations."

The airport now includes environmental aspects in all its planning.

"As a matter of fact, before you can build anything on an airport now, you've got to go through an environmental assessment. That in itself is a pretty expensive operation," General Moore noted.

Nashville remains committed to noise reduction. Aircraft noise is mitigated through the FAA-approved Airport Noise Compatibility Program, which began in 1986. The plan also projected that, thanks to advances in technology, aircraft noise will be reduced during the next decade. At the time the plan was approved, 58 percent of the aircraft using Nashville were Stage 3, which produce approximately 80 percent less noise than Stage 2 airplanes. The long-range plan projected that by 2003, all of the aircraft using the airport will be Stage 3, the quietest category of jet airplane.

Dealing With Crowded Airspace and Infrastructure

General Moore emphasized that the capacity of airports is the second major issue to be faced by aviation in the future. While he agreed with the decision to deregulate air service, this change has "brought on additional issues."

"When you look back now and you see the enormous difference in availability of air travel to our people, you know that it was the right decision," he stated. "There have been some adjustments required because of that. Airlines have been able with more flexibility to do things that marketing and free enterprise say you should do. And that's required some adjustments in the use of our facilities, airports and airspace.

"With more airplanes flying within the same amount of airspace, air traffic control becomes more difficult. And while we haven't found the final answers to this one yet, it's undoubtedly going to be the answer is you'll make better use of the airspace and the infrastructure that exists today.

"You can control the airspace by throwing enough resources into it, but I think there are practical limits, which say at some point you've got to spread the operations around a little bit," he advised. "You're beginning to see the airlines do more off-hub flying. And that's one of the reasons smaller aircraft, regional jets, are really coming into recognition and they're great in meeting the needs for which they are designed." The General proposed two ways to alleviate a capacity problem. One is to keep building facilities and capability at a location until it can handle whatever the traffic is.

The other way, he believes, is to use the infrastructure and airspace that already exists in this country.

"There are a number of airports that are overbuilt. Nashville, for example, was built to accommodate a hub. Today, we are in a position to handle additional traffic. I would say that one solution to the capacity issue is to use the facilities that exist. Put the traffic into airports that have capacity and relieve traffic at the large mega-hubs," General Moore said.

Another side to the capacity issue is reflected in the management styles of airlines, he explained. Airlines have to keep their unit costs down. And one way they do this is to put more units into whatever facility is supporting them.

"That means, you keep adding flights at the big hubs because that gives you your best unit cost solution," he added.

"Airlines are also market driven. They have tied their clientele to certain operations at convenient times. Passengers have become used to the schedule, and they don't want to change that. And I don't blame them," he acknowledged.

In the future, General Moore believes that due to delays and overbooking, airlines will look at airports like Nashville that can handle more flights.

"At the end of it, air service will continue to be the dominant form of domestic and international transportation. And the market for air service in the United States will continue to be the most dominant in the world. Many of our methods of operation may change because of the insane acts of terrorism inflicted upon us, but the basic soundness of our market and the resilient strength of our economic system will prevail. At that point, we will be wise to be on the way to reducing the congestion at mega-hubs and utilizing the unused capacity at our regional airports."

Eddie Jones agreed. "We've got to be on everybody's list when that time comes and I think it's coming. Chicago, New York, Boston, Atlanta, they're going to have to break some of that down. They're choking towns. And we've got the facilities, we're modern, well-run, and when they start slicing off chunks of that, Nashville is perfectly positioned to get some of that (service)."

As of March 2002, 15 airlines, including Southwest, which has made Nashville a "Focus" city, account for approximately 400 daily arrivals and departures. With room for additional service, the airport would expand the benefits it provides this community and region.

The inability to accurately predict future advances in technology, engineering and other sciences related to aviation, is a major change to airport planners.

So, too, is the type of service passengers will encounter when they arrive at the airport. In the past, airports were places where aircraft landed and took off and passengers could get some food as they arrived for or departed from their flights. Today's airports are shopping malls in the fullest sense offering diversified services and products to the business traveler, tourists, airport personnel and the community at large.

Robert Mathews predicted that in the next decade or two, "you're going to have an airport with no ticket counters." In fact, the age of ticketless travel is already here. In Europe, passengers simply go to a kiosk, swipe a credit card and get a boarding pass. They can strap a tag on their luggage, which is then put through a machine, he noted.

While Nashville International still functions around ticket counters, the European kiosk has arrived. In July 2001, American Airlines announced plans to open one of these one-stop kiosks at its ticket counter and two others at two gates at the airport. Passengers using a touch-screen can use a credit card to check in, change seat assignments, get boarding passes and check baggage.

Already, anyone with access to a computer and a credit card can log on and with a few clicks, make reservations and obtain a confirmation number – good for that next airline flight out of Nashville.

Ticketless travel has arrived. And no matter what other technological advances evolve in the future, the aviation adventure in Music City is poised to embrace the future because of the leadership of an exemplary airport staff working in tandem with equally capable members of the MNAA Board of Commissioners.

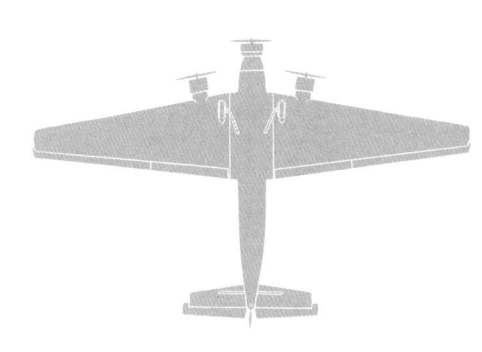

Giving Credit Where Credit is Due

Chapter 13

Chapter 13
Giving Credit Where Credit is Due

The vision of the MNAA Board of Commissioners continues in the tradition of the aviation pioneers who brought flight to Nashville and worked diligently to further the city's aviation adventure.

"This community could not afford to pay for the time, intelligence and talent provided by the volunteers who serve as members of our Board of Commissioners," Nelson Andrews said. "The management and staff of the airport, the local and national management of the airlines and the community at large are forever in the debt of each commissioner who has served on the Authority board."

While it is impossible to name all those who had a hand in the development of the Airport Authority and aviation in this region, some names do surface as noteworthy.

Central among these are those who served on the first Metropolitan Nashville Airport Authority board. The charter members of the MNAA board included John C. Tune, Jr., lawyer, pilot and MNAA's first chairman; AVCO engineer Harold Black; advertising executive William R. "Bill" Culbertson; realtor James L. Harper; Genesco chief Franklin Jarman; National Life & Accident Insurance's C.D. Walling, Jr.; and insurance executive David K. "Pat" Wilson.

Subsequent boards included businessman James T. Fulghum; attorney and one-time Lt. Governor of the state, Nashville attorney Frank Gorrell; The Mathews Group's Robert C.H. Mathews, Jr.; Life & Casualty's Alan Steele; investor Toby S. Wilt, and former chairman Mike Rose, to name just a few. These names surfaced repeatedly in discussions about those who contributed their leadership skills to the MNAA.

For example, Robert Mathews recalled that Frank Gorrell not only knew people all over the state but also in Washington, D.C., and truly understood human dynamics.

"He could size up a situation very quickly, and with incredible accuracy," Mathews said. "When the MNAA needed a first rate consultant to guide us through political and legal issues involved in domestic and international aviation, Frank was one of those who participated in the selection process. After listening to the presentations of a number of notable Washington law firms, Gorrell said, Mo Garfinkle is the only choice. From that point forward and for the next twelve years or so during which we worked with Mo and his colleagues, Frank's judgment was confirmed again and again."

"Frank was brilliant," Mathews added. "We engaged Mo Garfinkle who really helped us discipline our marketing strategy to the airlines and helped us to understand the air system and how it's changing. Mo's contacts are worldwide and we didn't know that at the time."

Nelson Andrews praised Pat Wilson's contributions. He acknowledged that without John (Tune) the MNAA "wouldn't have happened" but added," "Pat was a tremendous ingredient."

"I think you have to give Pat Wilson a lot of credit," he said. "You were beginning a new venture. You had to have the right players in place. One of the critical players was Pat Wilson. Pat is somebody who just doesn't ever take any credit. He just works in the background. He never tried to promote himself."

"Over the years, obviously "Bobby" Mathews has been a real trooper and a tremendous asset to the Authority," Andrews continued. "We've been really fortunate to have had those kinds of people."

Bob Hart, who worked closely with the MNAA in designing and building the new terminal, also singled out the board members he felt made valuable contributions.

"Bob Mathews and Pat Wilson – they had a way of making you feel that you just had to keep doing things better. 'That's good Bob, but, you know, make it better.' And so they were kind of inspiring people to work with. They had an attitude toward Nashville. Well, of course they thought it was a great place and they were able to express what they thought was really good about Nashville. That's what we tried to incorporate in the building," he explained.

"Board members like that are critical," Hart concluded.

"I think we're very fortunate that we've had Nashvillians that have been dedicated and given endless hours of their time to the Airport Authority," Dick Fulton said. He cited their service on the board plus their "leaving Nashville many, many times to visit other cities and airline offices to try to help increase the airline service in Nashville."

"So many people that were on those boards were really dedicated men. I just remember how extremely dedicated they were," Carolyn Tune recalled about the members who served with her late husband on the early MNAA board. "A couple of times we would go to international conferences and you would be traveling with them. And those men were really dedicated. They were taking time off to give a lot of time and attention to making it work," she added.

"There were a lot of men who were very bright and it was fun to be around them. It was just electric all the time."

Robert Mathews did follow John Tune onto the MNAA board. But his appointment in 1979 came about because of his business acumen.

Once Mathews got on the MNAA board, he used his vast business knowledge to enhance the Authority. Instead of the Airport Authority simply reacting to concerns that came in, he helped strengthen the Authority to reach out to the financial and planning communities, to the government and neighborhood groups.

This professional discipline of the corporation along with the market driven public sensitivity of an organization in dealing with the public were two pieces of magic Mathews brought to the Authority. In addition, he realized the importance of selecting the right people to serve.

One of the people Robert Mathews and Pat Wilson were instrumental in bringing on board was General William G. Moore, Jr.

"Relationships with airline executives were 'very, very important,'" according to Wilson, "and that's where General Moore shone."

Richard Fulton agreed.

"I don't know of anyone who could have done the job that he has done in leading the development of the Nashville airline services," the former mayor said. "I don't know of any airport director that could have been any better for development of the airport than General Moore. We're just so fortunate to have had the benefit of his services. I just can't say enough about how good he has been for the city."

Bob Hart recognized that the General's leadership abilities were critical to the process of building the new terminal.

"He is again one of those extraordinary people that Nashville was fortunate to have at that place at that time," Hart declared. "He was a leader who had a way of setting things up so people could do their jobs. I guess that's what generals are good at. He recognized what each of us could do and he created the conditions that helped us do it."

"I think Bill Moore is one of the best that's ever been," Nelson Andrews believed. "You knew that he wasn't going to let it (the airport) deteriorate, that as you needed things, he was going to make it happen."

Andrews noted it would have been easy not to do the work that's been done at the airport in the last couple of years. "He'd always say, 'now, here's what's happening. Here's what's coming down the road. Here's what our projections are, so we must do these things.'"

One example Andrews cited is the overflow parking lot. While it is needed only some of the time now, the General recognized that in time it probably will be needed all of the time, so they needed to get ahead of the flow.

A pilot himself, Andrews appreciated General Moore's efforts to ease traffic at Nashville International by expanding the John Tune Airport for general aviation.

"He did understand that. The Tune Airport took a lot of pressure off the big airport because obviously, you've got all the airlines flying in there. There are a whole lot of little planes going in and out of there. If you can take some of those planes out of that process, then that keeps you from having delays and backups and so many people on the runways. So that made a lot of sense," Andrews said.

Another of the former MNAA president's strengths was his connection in Washington, D.C. Pat Wilson recalled the General's efforts with federal officials to get a new runway built.

"I remember so well somebody told me, 'you know, when you go to Washington with General Moore you never have to sit and wait.' They were ready for him. He was held in such high regard," Wilson added.

"I really think the phenomenal growth that Nashville has experienced over the last two decades, in my estimation, can be laid right at the feet of General Moore," he added. "Without that airport that General Moore is responsible for, we'd still be a second tier city in my estimation, and we're not anymore. We're a first tier city. There's no question about that."

Hospitality executive Jack Vaughn also cited good freight service the General worked so hard to provide as a reason conventions like to come to Nashville.

Vaughn has heard a lot of positive comments from visitors coming into the Gaylord Opryland Resort and Convention Center about the Southern hospitality at the airport.

"General Moore created an atmosphere out there that is probably very unique. I always felt that there was a lot of Southern hospitality and warmth in the way you're treated out at that airport. There's a little touch there that I'm really glad to see," E.W. Wendell said.

"Everybody's impressed with him," Wendell acknowledged. "He has done so much for this community.

"Just on the strength of his personality, he gathered community support. And everybody respected him so, that if he said it was so, you believed it. You knew it was right. He was a very forceful individual. And I don't think an airport could be even modestly successful if it didn't have the support of the community and the business community."

"He had just about 100 percent support from the business community, from the Chamber of Commerce," Fulton added. "Certainly when I was mayor he had my support."

The General was "wonderful with the community," Pat Wilson noted and added that his leadership skills made Wilson's job on the board easier. "There aren't many four-star generals with worldwide aviation experience and great administrative abilities and a helluva fine personality."

Nelson Andrews also credited General Moore with being an integral part of the general and business communities.

Andrews commented that the General could have said, "all I've got to do is run the airport. I don't care about anything else," but instead, "he's been involved in a lot of different things that weren't just 100 percent airport."

Fulton said, "we were just fortunate to have had him."

"If there's ever been a hero of aviation in this community, it was John Tune," Andrews said of the lawyer and pilot who dreamed of creating an Airport Authority for his native Nashville and Middle Tennessee.

"He's the one who got it done," Andrews stated. "He was really remarkable. I keep a mental list of what I think are the Top 10 things that people have done in a sort of volunteer capacity in this community and he is still in that Top 10 and pretty high up after all this time."

Another who agreed that John Tune was "tremendously instrumental" in getting an Airport Authority for the city is Eddie Jones.

"He had a passion for it. Of course, he was a pilot and he loved aviation and he just wanted to see Nashville's airport become a showcase for the city and have the level of service to support that kind of a facility," Jones recalled. "He really was a visionary and tenacious – just night and day. I think he had to kind of quit practicing law for awhile to devote almost all of his time to making this happen."

Another who saw Tune as a visionary is Robert Mathews.

"John Tune said things a lot of times that proved to be right. He was a visionary. He was really committed to the community; was president of the Chamber. He felt he owed something to the community and I don't know why. The community never did anything for him."

When John Tune died on April 13, 1983, at age 51 following a long battle with cancer, the Nashville Banner noted that he had led the move to establish the Metropolitan Airport Authority and had crusaded for quality over quantity in Nashville's growth. The MNAA's first chairman, Tune served in that capacity twice and was a commissioner until his death.

"I have realized so much more so since John died really what a breadth of vision he had," his widow Carolyn Tune noted. "As I reflect back on it, it's just amazing the vision he had.

"He was always thinking years ahead of time. He had just a really great ability to see things from 'the big picture' as he would say.

"We're talking about a man who when we first married was running his father's Buick dealership. And he came home one afternoon and he said, 'you know, I really think that I need to feel like I have done my own thing. So he wanted to go into the used car business."

He turned to friends for financial support and opened a used car business down on Broadway in an empty space between two brick buildings. His business had no glass front. He paid back his investors in less than two years. Not long after that, an import franchise became available. At that time, nobody was driving imports, but Tune bought this import line and his used car business became an import dealership, selling mostly British cars. Thanks to his breadth of vision, he realized Toyota was going to be a big seller and sold the British line and took on Toyota and Volvo.

When one of his brothers-in-law started night law school, he heeded the advice of his father-in-law who was an attorney and enrolled in night law school as well.

While studying law at night, he continued to run his car business and fly for the National Guard. He loved law school and when he finished he decided to practice law.

Carolyn Tune recalled this time in their life.

"We had three children, and he came home and said, 'you know, we might starve to death but I'm going to get somebody to run my car business. I'm going to practice law.' It never ever occurred to me to be worried because he knew what he wanted to do and he knew he wanted to do it on his own," she added.

The Airport Authority "was just something that he thought needed to be done and he enjoyed it," she surmised.

"He had been in business and so he really understood the business world very well, having just been out there in the real world. And then he had the legal background and he certainly had the aviation background so they all came together as natural loves and interests for him," she added.

The concept of an Airport Authority came about as a result of his love for people, the community, economics, the law and especially flying.

Carolyn Tune noted that all three of their sons, David, Julian and John Edward "Jet," learned to fly like their father. In fact, she added, all those who had a close relationship with John would end up taking flying lessons. Even his partner in the automobile business got his pilot's license. "I think everybody that was around him just caught that flying fever from him," she said.

One of those was Eddie Jones.

"John Tune was a super salesman. He was, of course, tremendously knowledgeable of his subject and he loved to fly," Jones recalled. "John and a couple of others had bought a light plane and I was going out in the afternoons and flying with John and just had a great time with him. I had been a World War II fighter pilot and John enjoyed bringing me up-to-date.

"And he had all sorts of credibility in town and didn't ever want to do anything except what's right and what's good for the airport and good for the city. And if it met those tests, it was fine with John Tune. Everybody believed that. I believed it," Jones said.

Nelson Andrews also believed that.

"He was so far ahead of a lot of us," Andrews recalled. "He envisioned that we were going to be international."

Although international air service is limited now, Andrews agreed with Tune's vision that maybe that day will come too.

Another thing down the road, is Nashville's becoming a bigger distribution center.

"He talked about that. He had just a remarkable vision of what was going to happen. All those kinds of things tie in. If we did become a big distribution center, then you've got to say, 'What's the impact of that on the airport?' We're so centrally located in terms of the Eastern half of the United States and its population that you take all of that into consideration," Andrews added.

John Tune also envisioned the airport becoming a regional one, Andrews recalled.

"He really did. He didn't see it in the Southwest sort of thing but he did see that when you've got more routes and more ways for people to go some place, that the more you do, the more of a mass you have," he continued.

As more opportunities in air service developed, Tune envisioned a lot of people driving to Nashville to fly out of the airport here rather than some place else.

"We talked about Chattanooga. He said, 'Chattanooga probably will never have a great airport as long as we're dominant. A lot of people will come here.' And it's true. They will," Andrews stressed.

John Tune's efforts on behalf of the MNAA ended when he died in 1983.

"It was a tremendous loss to Nashville and to everyone to have John leave us at such an early age. He was a major force in bringing about the new airport and of course, as you know, the airport out at Cockrill Bend is the John C. Tune Airport and that has been a big asset to Nashville," Richard Fulton declared.

"We were good friends," Fulton continued. "John was one who also played a role in influencing me to leave Congress and come back and be mayor."

When John Tune died, Fulton had, in fact, wanted to rename the Nashville Municipal Airport for him.

"When John died, Dick Fulton called and said, 'I really would like to ask the Metro Council to rename the airport for John,'" Carolyn Tune remembered. "I'm sure you know that every airport has its call name or whatever you call that on maps. Nashville is BNA for Berry Field Nashville. I thought how many people know that the terminal has this name or that the airport has this name. I felt like it was important for it to retain Nashville in its name, and also, I couldn't envision them changing maps all through the aeronautical industry," Carolyn Tune recalled. "It just didn't make sense to me."

"I knew that this fixed base operation had been his dream," she continued. "And I said, 'Well, you know, Dick, rather than do that, if you're asking me for my choice, I think it would mean more to John to have the fixed base operation named for him. And that way they would never have to change any charts and it wouldn't cost taxpayers money to go through and do all that.'"

When the city's new general aviation airport opened in 1986, it went on aeronautical charts and maps as John C. Tune Airport and is now a great source of pride for John Tune's family. "He was a hero to me in every way," said Carolyn Tune when asked if her late husband could be called a hero of aviation.

Many credit him with being the father of the MNAA and insist it wouldn't have happened without him.

"I think he was the architect really and rightfully he gets the credit as being the architect for the Airport Authority and for the success it's had," agreed E. W. Wendell. "I think everybody who knew John would say, 'He's the man.' Everybody else just followed through on the plan he set up."

"I think that John Tune should be given credit for having been very much of a visionary, but not just a visionary but someone who was able to implement the vision. He was able to bring about the reality of the vision he had," Dick Fulton concluded.

The MNAA—a Model Airport Authority

Chapter 14

Chapter 14
The MNAA—a Model Airport Authority

John Tune's vision of an Airport Authority was one free of politics and one that took advantage of talented individuals with expertise in a variety of disciplines related to aviation. He wanted an independent entity that was run like a business. Such a structure, he envisioned, would provide definite advantages in dealing with the airlines, dealing with and drawing support from the community and region and dealing with the local, state and federal levels of government.

Through sheer determination and with help from like-minded citizens, John Tune sold this concept to the local and state leaders and the Metropolitan Nashville Airport Authority was born. With the airlines' backing, the MNAA paid off bonds and bought the airport from the city.

Consequently, unlike other airports that are owned and operated by city government, Nashville's airport is mostly independent as an instrument of Metro Government.

It is run by the non-profit MNAA for the benefit of the community. All revenues are put back into the airport structure. The budget has input from the airlines. The FAA has strict guidelines for how money that comes from ticket taxes is spent.

The structure does have a system of checks and balances built in at the local level. The mayor appoints and Metro Council approves board members, thus allowing government input. However, members must represent specified disciplines related to aviation and business.

Other checks and balances are built in also. For example, the state charter does not give the Airport Authority the power of condemnation that the government has. The Authority has to go through the system like private enterprise does to get approval and have the city buy in to plans such as land use changes.

One advantage, however, is that the MNAA charter is, like the Constitution, a flexible document. While the basic precepts stay the same, over time it can be adapted and changed as needed.

Robert Mathews pointed out that when the Airport Authority concept was formed, the enabling act did not specify gender or racial representation. Then, when the American Airlines hub came in, the MNAA didn't have a neighborhood representative on the board to deal with the noise issue. To remedy this, MNAA went back to the state legislature to get the law amended.

As a result, the MNAA went from a seven-member to a 10-member Board of Commissioners. Today, Nashville's Airport Authority consists of three (3) business and finance representatives, two (2) pilot representatives, two (2) neighborhood representatives, one (1) engineer representative, one (1) legal representative and the mayor of Nashville/Davidson County.

As always, board members are not paid for their services.

"Since the original Authority, it's been tweaked a time or two to add representation from the minority community and to be gender sensitive," Eddie Jones added.

The Board of Commissioners also asks its members to serve on specific committees aligned with the various MNAA departments.

This additional committee substructure to the MNAA board came after careful study.

Keeping Politics to the Minimum

Nelson Andrews cautioned against too many unnecessary political changes to the concept that John Tune envisioned of a non-political Airport Authority.

"I think what you want from an Airport Authority are good citizens who have a sense of numbers because these are big numbers, who understand finance, who understand the process of airlines, who understand the economic factors involved in an airport, who are really broad-based. I think it's a broad-based enterprise and you ought to have broad-based people involved in it."

"While I was mayor I was criticized sometimes by some of my Democratic friends – I was elected to Congress as a Democrat and I am a Democrat – when it came time to make appointments to the Airport Authority," Dick Fulton recalled. "I made sure that we recommended to the Metro Council, that had to approve the appointments, people that I felt would be a tremendous asset to the continued growth and development of air transportation in Nashville and Middle Tennessee."

He admitted he appointed some Republicans and some Democrats and some he never knew which party they belonged to.

"During my predecessor Beverly Briley's administration and my administration, I'm not sure what happened in other administrations, I don't recall ever calling a member of the Airport Authority or the director of the airport and attempting to use political influence in any of the decisions they were making," Fulton added.

Mathews also thought the idea of structuring the board to include members with specific areas of expertise was ingenious.

"Each individual appointed to the board has to bring something to the table that is knowledgeable and meaningful to the Airport Authority," he explained.

For example, he pointed out that Frank Gorrell's knowledge of the political and legal systems was invaluable to the MNAA as was Pat Wilson's understanding of economics and the environment. "Mathews himself is an example of an individual who brought a tremendous knowledge of real estate and the construction business," said Fulton.

The MNAA structure has worked well for Nashville also because business leaders in the community support it. One reason they view it so favorably is because of its independence.

"The mayor does appoint its members, but the airport borrows money and it's not part of the Metropolitan government's budget," Pat Wilson noted, adding, "independent financing is a better way of saying it."

"The business leadership of the City of Nashville is very comfortable and supportive of the leadership and authority of the Authority. There's no tax money in this deal anywhere. And it takes a pretty skilled group of business-oriented people to make that operation run and prosper and grow," Eddie Jones stressed.

"I know for a fact, leadership within the airline industry and the hospitality industry, both of those two groups, feel like Nashville is a good pioneer city in terms of how it handles, manages, runs and grows its air facilities and services," he added.

E.W. Wendell is another businessman who believed in the MNAA's structure.

"That's a novel way to do it in my judgment – a unique way to do it – to have an independent agency out here away from the political agendas," he declared.

"Our type of organization, our charter – the fact that we are an independent operation, that we have reduced the political effects on our operation – allows us to focus on the things that are important that other people may not understand are important," Wendell said.

"I don't believe you can achieve the necessary level of commitment on the part of an Airport Authority if it doesn't have the freedom and flexibility and support that it needs to continue to strive for an excellent operation," he added.

Jack Vaughn, who had numerous business dealings with the MNAA regarding the then Opryland Hotel and Convention Center, appreciated the Authority's efficient, business-like operation that is free of politics. He agreed one hundred percent with the MNAA structure, adding, "I hope they never change that simply because it is run like a business."

Vaughn especially liked the fact that members are selected because of their business acumen.

"That's what is so wonderful," he added. As for any changes, he quickly replied, "It's one of those 'If it ain't broke, don't fix it.'"

Eddie Jones also felt the business-like structure of the MNAA lends itself very well to being able to work well with the airlines.

"It has credibility. It has no ax to grind. I've never known of anybody on the Authority then or now who's attempted to use it for any sort of political purposes. It's purely a business. And airlines themselves are big business and they're dealing with a group that understands and comes from the private sector of the business world. It has great credibility and acceptance."

When American Airlines approached the MNAA about putting a hub in Nashville and needed some assurances rather quickly, the board was able to respond in less than a month.

"Here was an example of a local political body run by a mayor, who could do certain things, and the MNAA, a non-profit entity represented by community leaders and a president, who also could get things done in a hurry and on time," Mathews declared.

"We all joined hands and could react quickly to this request of this airline. Otherwise, we wouldn't have gotten the American Airlines hub in here," he pointed out.

The ability to act quickly also paid off in redesigning a portion of the new terminal to accommodate American Airlines.

Design for the new building was almost finished when American approached about adding a hub. American came in and designed and paid for changes to its wing.

"That's how we ended up with an Admirals Club and the way the terminal was laid out with a bend on the C and D concourses," Mathews revealed. "It was all designed by American and paid for by American.

"I say at this airport, we've had great community support. Certainly there was a time when most people didn't understand either the extent of the nuisance of the airport or the great economic opportunity that a developed airport presents to the community. So we had some opposition but that has long since faded away to practically nothing today."

Nelson Andrews agreed that community support is imperative for many reasons.

"If the Chamber ever got down on the airport, it would be the kiss of death," he stated. "You always have the issue of noise and that sort of thing that you have to deal with. You think you don't have to deal with airlines but I think it takes community support basically even with them. They need to know that we're all still for a strong airport and we're going to be supportive and not going to let it deteriorate."

To ensure continued support both now and in the future, the MNAA embarked on an effort to make the community a part of the airport and this operation. To accomplish this, they included the community in the airport's long-range planning.

"The FAA required us to do a long-range plan and update it every five years," the General explained. "We had done one several years ago. When we undertook this long-range plan, we decided we would go out 30 years instead of the 20 years, which the FAA required at that time. That is so that we could encompass all of the development that we could foresee at that time on the airport in that plan."

"Then we went out to the whole community. We broadcast it on TV. We put it in the papers. There were drawings. I personally made, my staff tells me, about 60 or 70 presentations around the community here to whomever wanted to listen to be sure that everybody understood what we were shooting for in the future, where we were going and why. I think that helped us a lot in getting the kind of community support that we have achieved."

Just as the MNAA has been aware of the need to work closely with the community, it also is cognizant of the need to work well with government. Consequently, the MNAA has formed a good working relationship with government at all levels – local, state and federal.

The state law that set up the Airport Authority, according to Robert Mathews, required that the MNAA should work with the Metro Council and the planning commission as any private, non-profit entity does.

"So you didn't have an attitude of 'We can just do what we want to,'" he pointed out.

The MNAA also maintains a good working relationship with the State of Tennessee, particularly in dealing with time consuming road projects. Donelson Pike, a state route, had to be relocated before the new terminal could be built and this project could have delayed construction but didn't.

A good relationship with the federal government is critical because of FAA funding and regulation. In the past, the MNAA needed help from the federal government in a timely manner on issues involving noise mitigation and federal funding for the new runway. The MNAA was a pacesetter in this nation in getting the Noise Mitigation Act and the Letter of Intent program approved by the federal government.

The MNAA's structure helped speed up the negotiation process at both the local and federal levels.

"A key at this end was the support we were getting from the city, which, of course, went right to the politicians. "We had the political support that we needed, and if there's one thing that the FAA is attuned to it is politics. With that, and I think we had a very persuasive story, we were able to present our case and they accepted it. And everybody went to work and got on the team to build a runway."

The structure of the organization helped here as well, the General agreed.

When told "you can't do this" or "you can't do that," the engineers, pilots, real estate developers and community representatives on the board could reply, "yes, it can be done."

Their input indeed helped, the General added. "We were really pulling together as a team."

General Moore pointed out that the Noise Mitigation Act and the Letter of Intent Program opened the door for a lot of airports.

Thanks to Nashville's Airport Authority, many airports were able to do things they had not been able to do before. And the Noise Reimbursement Act did the same thing on the noise side and on the community support side.

The Letter of Intent program expanded so rapidly, the FAA put a cap on it," he recalled. "They would only take so many of those programs."

The General was amazed at the popularity of the programs once the MNAA got them in place.

"If you stop and think about it, we're not the first airport in the country with these issues. A lot of airports had been needing runways and noise mitigation and so on before we ever arrived on the scene in that sense. Why somebody hadn't gotten both of those programs years before we did, I don't know," he declared.

Fortunately, the MNAA was intellectually free and had the corporate flexibility to think of these solutions to these issues.

"We don't rely on the city for taxes to support us. We support ourselves. Yet all the benefits of having an airport go to the city," he stressed. "I think it's the best of all worlds. We are able to avoid a lot of pitfalls and hurdles with the kind of organization that we have."

At the recommendation of the airlines, other cities have studied Nashville's Airport Authority as a model airport governance form.

"We didn't advertise ourselves as a model," General Moore said. "Other cities said, 'Hey, we've got a model down there. Let's go see if we can copy it.'"

What they are seeing is the creation of "one of the real visionaries that was probably the spark plug in getting this Authority going years ago," he explained. "John Tune's driving force was the conviction that we had to get that airport out of politics and get it into the business world. And that is what we have now with minimal political interference."

Eddie Jones recalled that several other cities, not too long after the MNAA was created started going the airline authority route as a way for a city to handle its air service.

"I know that other cities have been through here and looked at the Airport Authority," he added. "I don't know what the outcome was, but for some reason I remember a delegation from Lexington, Kentucky, that came here and spent a couple of days looking at Metropolitan government in general and the Airport Authority in particular. And Nashville's Metropolitan government is a model, and other cities that have come in to study that almost always have spent some time and asked, 'Tell me about this airport deal. How does it work?'"

Nelson Andrews agreed that interest in Metropolitan Nashville's form of city-county government has contributed to interest in the MNAA. He also fielded some calls about the Airport Authority from officials in other cities who knew he had a role in its formation.

More recently, Robert Mathews in his former role as board chairman has talked with numerous government and airport officials in cities such as Jackson, Miss.; Birmingham, Ala.; and Atlanta, Ga., (which is a regional airport but is owned by the city).

Mathews noted that a lot of airports sought guidance and modeling after Nashville even though they are still owned by the city and don't have the Airport Authority system.

"In fact," he added, "the government of Canada, which controls the airlines, has decided to decentralize and has come to look at a model of how to set it up."

While government officials are looking at Nashville's model governance system, they're also looking at the city's modern airport terminal, which exists today in large part due to the MNAA.

Not only has the MNAA been a model, Nashville International Airport has served as a model for other airports as well and has helped foster a new trend in airport design, according to project lead design architect Bob Hart.

Hart is equally certain that the MNAA's structure as a non-political, self-supporting entity helped the design team achieve its goals.

"John Tune's vision was a very healthy vision for Nashville when it came to building the terminal as well as running it," Hart is convinced.

"The board could concentrate and did concentrate on what is the best airport, the best functional airport for this community and what is the best look and the best expression of this community, the best kind of landmark. They could do that without considering anything but the airport itself and the people of Nashville. There was no other agenda other than the airport," the designer noted.

"We take a lot of credit, being the architects, because we're the ones who draw the drawings, but to do a good building, it takes a great client in the sense that they know what they want and they're organized in a way that they're able to get it. And they were."

"The MNAA board formed a unified client – a client who knew what they wanted and knew how to help us create it, he added."

Without hidden agendas, delays, distractions or irrelevant matters, the design team was able to focus on the function of the place and the cost and the look of it.

Having worked with a number of public and political bodies, Hart is convinced that working with an Authority whose members may be politically appointed but are experts with real talent and one that is independent of the political process is clearly the best way to build buildings like an airport.

Another major advantage of any Airport Authority like Nashville's is its longevity, according to Hart, who worked with the MNAA on the airport's long-term 30-year Master Plan.

"And again, an Authority can take that on," he said of the airport's plan for the future. "Those kinds of plans take 10 or 20 years to accomplish and an Authority can often do that with more consistency than a political body with a lot of other agendas can."

Managing an airport is a long-term project and the political system isn't set up to manage long-term projects.

"It (an airport) requires the horizon for planning and developing over a 10 to 20 year period. The political system is set for change every two to four years. It's difficult for a political entity to manage airports," he reasoned.

"Airports are operating in a highly competitive aviation industry," he continued. "Certain business requirements are extremely important in managing an airport. The board and staff need qualifications that aren't required of city employees. It takes a more specialized board and specialized staff to run an airport."

"This is the wisdom of John Tune," Hart concluded.

Aviation has changed markedly in the past century not just in Nashville but around the world. Advances in technology and the development of commercial aviation first in a regulated environment and then a deregulated one, have contributed to this change.

Air service has grown and airports have grown to keep up with the demand. Nashville is not unlike other cities that have watched as its airport has grown and prospered. However, all those who contributed to this history agreed that Nashville has done a better job than most other airports, thanks to a very unique group of individuals and a unique form of governance.

The Metropolitan Nashville Airport Authority clearly was the right form of governance at the right time for the City of Nashville. It did exactly what John Tune envisioned. It removed the airport from the political process and allowed it to be run as an independent business. The airport has developed into a first-class facility – and air service has flourished. As a result of this very workable structure, the City of Nashville and the Middle Tennessee region have grown and prospered.

"Somehow the forefathers here were very smart," E. W. Wendell volunteered.

It was a tough decision for Nashville Mayor Beverly Briley to support the creation of the MNAA and the sale of the airport to the Authority, Dick Fulton acknowledged. As far as he knows, no one approached Briley to reverse his decision.

"Briley must have put an end to that," he added.

Neither Fulton nor any of the other community-minded citizens who shared this vision have been inclined to tamper with the Airport Authority concept.

"Obviously, the results show that it does work," Fulton agreed. "And what do they say, 'If it's not broken, don't fix it.'"

"I'm ashamed to say I cannot name all the members of the Airport Authority now, but I know two or three and I think you will find that as a group they will still represent the key areas that they need to have expertise in," Eddie Jones declared. "And they have an experience level that will travel with them in terms of providing the continuity and having historical perspective and background – a sense of what has happened in the past to help you decide what to do in the future."

"That group will have a lot of support if it needs it and asks for it from the community at large because there's a tremendous amount of respect for the Authority as an organization," Jones added. "There are people in the community who support the Authority who probably have never met a member of it. There's an image of the Authority, well deserved, as a good thing for the city. You don't need to tie that to specific members."

The many others who have worked diligently to ensure the success of this concept are in agreement, and today John Tune's vision lives on.

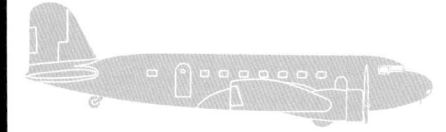

A Time of Transition

Chapter 15

Chapter 15
A Time of Transition

After heading the MNAA for 17 years, General Moore announced that he would retire in 2001. The MNAA commissioners designated one of their members, Fred Dettwiller, to chair a search committee to find a replacement for General Moore.

After an exhaustive study of qualified candidates and a number of personal interviews, Dettwiller's committee recommended that the board offer the position to Raul L. Regalado, who had an impressive background in aviation. The board supported the recommendation of the search committee.

There followed meetings between the MNAA commissioners and Regalado, who accepted the position and became President and CEO of MNAA on April 9, 2001.

Regalado was the deputy director of aviation for the City of Houston, Texas, and served as chief operating officer for George Bush International and Houston Hobby Airports, as well as Ellington Field. Houston's international airport operations involved 27 million domestic passengers, three million international passengers and more than 300,000 tons of cargo annually.

He has served as the director of aviation for the City of San Jose, responsible for the San Jose International Airport and other airports in Orange County and Fresno, California, and in Klamath Falls, Oregon. From 1995 to 1998, he was the market president of national sales for APCOA, Inc., an international parking company.

The new president is a veteran of the United States Army and is a former member of the California Army National Guard and the U.S. Army Reserve. He is the recipient of numerous military awards and citations, including The Legion of Merit, the Distinguished Flying Cross, Bronze Star, the Air Medal for Valor and forty-nine Air Medals for combat missions.

He holds a Bachelor of Science degree in aviation management from Embry-Riddle Aeronautical University and has completed an extensive range of educational programs in the military. He is a commercial pilot and a member of the American Association of Airport Executives, the Airport Minority Advisory Council and the Retired Officers Association.

In late 2000, airports were beginning to feel the pinch of an economic contraction in which corporate, tourist and personal travel were declining sharply. The downward ticks were measured in every important category: passenger facility charges, landing fees, concessions, parking and tenant revenues. By mid-2001, Dettwiller and other board members knew the facts well and had projected the trends. They were prepared to shape policies empowering the Authority's management, led by Regalado, to take the actions necessary to ensure the competitive position of Nashville in domestic and world markets and to continue the sustained growth of passenger service to and from the city.

Everyone knew it was going to be tough. No one knew just how tough.

Terrorism Forever Changes Aviation

The unthinkable happened on a clear, blue morning of September 11, as history has recorded but the world has yet to fully understand. Two commercial airliners were used by fanatical terrorists as bombs to devastate the lives of thousands and destroy the twin towers of the World Trade Center in New York City. A third aircraft struck the Pentagon in Washington, D.C., again wreaking death and destruction. A fourth attempt was cut short by the courageous acts of passengers who forced the aircraft to crash in Pennsylvania, giving their lives, to prevent additional carnage.

Reactions were instantaneous.

The Federal Aviation Administration ordered 4,873 private and commercial aircraft grounded immediately. In less than two hours, the sky over America was empty again just as it was before the first flight almost a century ago.

Never before had domestic and international air transportation been grounded in the United States. Never before had one sector of the private enterprise been singled out for vicious attack. Never before had issues come thundering down on airports as they did during the days and weeks immediately following the death and destruction of New York City and Washington.

In fact, many of the decisions, beginning in those first crushing moments and continuing through the next 36 hours, were made by Raul Regalado and other key members of his management team who were not in Nashville at the time of the attack. They were forced to the ground along with the rest of the nation and had to return by charter jet from an international business conference they were attending in Canada.

The Metropolitan Nashville Airport Authority's commissioners and management sprang into action and worked to ensure the safety of the people and property for which they were responsible. As soon as the FAA lifted the ban on flying, Nashville International Airport opened again for business.

Many of the Nashville community would later reflect that, as the hours flew by, the MNAA functioned like a private sector company capable of quick decisions and decisive action.

In a very real sense, that ability to think and act as a business serving the interests of air passengers, the aviation industry and the Nashville community-at-large is the essence of what the Metropolitan Nashville Airport Authority was designed to do and what it has been doing consistently since its inception in 1970. The strength of this unique authority concept remains intact and poised to handle whatever challenges the future holds. Indeed, John Tune's vision lives on and bodes well for the 21st century.

The history of the Metropolitan Nashville Airport Authority and its predictions for the future changed drastically on September 11, 2001. And while aviation's great adventure took a deadly turn that day. . .it did not come to a halt. Just like those massive jetliners that now have returned to the skies, the aviation adventure in Nashville, Tennessee, and the world soars once again.

Appendixes

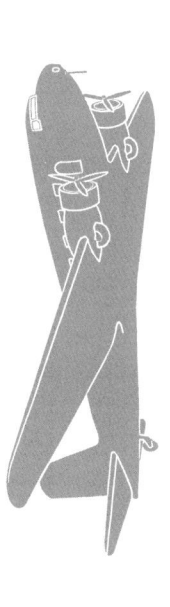

APPENDIX A

METROPOLITAN NASHVILLE AIRPORT AUTHORITY BOARD CHAIRMAN

January 1972 - April 1973
   John C. Tune, Jr.
May 1973 - April 1976
   Harold J. Black
May 1976 - August 1979
   C.D. Walling
September 1979 - June 1980
   Harold J. Black
July 1980 - November 1982
   John C. Tune, Jr.
December 1982 - March 2001
   Robert C.H. Matthews, Jr.
April 2001 - May 2002
   G. Fred Dettwiller
June 2002 - May 2003
   R. Clayton McWhorter
June 2003 - Present
   James H. Cheek, III

EXECUTIVE OFFICER/PRESIDENTS

1970 - 1972
   C.W. (Ted) Flowers
April 1972 - July 1972
   James Graham (Acting)
August 1972 - January 1977
   Albert Huber
February 1977 - January 1981
   James Graham
February 1981 - May 1981
   Steve Fitzhugh (Acting)
June 1981 - March 1984
   Richard Price
April 1984 - March 2001
   Gen. William Moore
April 2001 - Present
   Raul L. Regalado

METROPOLITAN NASHVILLE AIRPORT AUTHORITY BOARD OF COMMISSIONERS

1970 CHARTER MEMBERS

   John C. Tune, Jr., MNAA chairman
   C.D. Walling, Jr.
   David K. "Pat" Wilson
   Harold J. Black
   Franklin Jarman
   James L. Harper
   William R. Culbertson

MEMBERS JUNE 2003 - PRESENT

   James H. Cheek III, chairman
   J.D. Elliot, vice chairman
   Mayor Bill Purcell
   Ann V. Butterworth
   Betty J. Marshall
   Bert Mathews
   The Honorable Gilbert S. Merritt
   Juli H. Mosley
   Irby Simpkins, Jr.
   Jack Bovender

APPENDIX B

BIBLIOGRAPHY/SOURCES

THE BEGINNINGS
Interview with:
Robert C.H. Mathews, Jr.
Written sources:
Encyclopedia Americana (Grolier Inc., Danbury, Conn., 2000)
"Famous Firsts in Aviation," *Information Please 1988 Almanac* (Houghton Mifflin Company, Boston, MA, 1988)
Tennessean: November 4, 1936

INTRODUCTION
Interviews with:
Nelson Andrews, Richard Fulton, Edward F. "Eddie" Jones, Robert C.H. Mathews, Jr., E. W. "Bud" Wendell, Jack Vaughn
Written source:
"McConnell to Cole to Berry," presentation by Robert C.H. Mathews, Jr., to the Coffee House Club, May 16, 1991
Web site:
www.news.iwon.com -
"NASA Unveils New Plane, Calls It Future of Aviation," Reuters, April 18, 2001

CHAPTER 1
Written sources:
Aviation in Tennessee by Jim Fulbright (Mid-South Publications, Goodlettsville, Tenn., c1998)
Green Hills News, April 19, 1990
Early History of Nashville by Lizzie P. Elliott (Tennessee Book Company, 1967; originally published by the Board of Education, Nashville, 1911)

Encyclopedia Americana (Grolier Inc., Danbury, Conn., 2000)
Information Please 1988 Almanac (Houghton Mifflin Company, Boston, Mass., 1988)
Nashville AreaWide WonderBook (Mast Advertising, CGC Publishing, Miamisburg, Ohio, 2000, 2001)
Nashville, 1780-1860: From Frontier to City by Anita Shafer Goodstein (University of Florida Press, Gainesville, Fla, 1989)
Nashville Banner: Aug. 25, 1935; June 13, 1937
Nashville: The Faces of Two Centuries, 1780-1980, written and edited by John Egerton (Produced by Nashville! Magazine, Plus Media, Inc., 1979)
Tennessean: Dec. 2, 1928; Sept. 23, 1987; July 4, 2001
World Book Encyclopedia (World Book Inc., Chicago, Ill, 2001)
Web sites:
www.faa.gov - "A Brief History of the Federal Aviation Administration"
www.library.nashville.org - Nashville, Davidson County Time Line, January 1996
www.nashintl.com (Nashville International Airport)

CHAPTER 2

Interview with: Nelson Andrews

Written sources:

Aviation in Tennessee by Jim Fulbright (Mid-South Publications, Goodlettsville, Tenn., C1998)

Encyclopedia Americana (Grolier Inc., Danbury, Conn., 2000)

Fortunes, Fiddles & Fried Chicken – A Nashville Business History by Bill Carey (Hillsboro Press, Franklin, Tenn., 2000)

"McConnell to Cole to Berry," presentation by Robert C.H. Mathews, Jr., to the Coffee House Club, May 16, 1991

Nashville AreaWide WonderBook (Mast Advertising, CGC Publishing, Miamisburg, Ohio, 2000, 2001)

Nashville Banner: March 15, 1936; Nov. 1, 1936; June 13, 1937; Sept. 28, 1938; Oct. 24, 1961

Nashville Clubs & Organizations, circa 1952

Nashville in the New South. 1880-1930 by Don H. Doyle (University of Tennessee Press, Knoxville, Tenn., 1985)

Nashville Scene, "I Remember Nashville" by George Boyles, 1989

Nashville: The Faces of Two Centuries, 1780-1980, written and edited by John Egerton (Produced by Nashville! Magazine, Plus Media Inc., 1979)

Official Program "Opening Municipal Airport," June 13, 1937

Tennessean: Dec. 12, 1934; Feb. 6, 1935; April 6, 1936; June 24 and 25, 1936; Sept. 20, 1936; Oct. 8, 1936; Nov. 1, 1936; Nov. 2, 1936; June 11, 1937; June 13, 1937; June 14, 1937; Nov. 7, 1937; Sept. 28, 1940; Nov. 4, 1987

"Blackwood Field to Berry Field, 1921 to 1986," Tennessee National Guard 65th Anniversary edition, 1986

World Book Encyclopedia (World Book Inc., Chicago, Ill, 2001)

CHAPTER 3

Interviews with:

Gen. William G. Moore, Jr., Carolyn Tune

Written sources:

Aviation in Tennessee by Jim Fulbright (Mid-South Publications, Goodlettsville, Tenn., C1998)

Nashville: The Faces of Two Centuries, 1780-1980, written and edited by John Egerton (Produced by Nashville! Magazine, Plus media Inc., 1979)

Review of the book *Daughter of The Air: The Brief Soaring Life of Cornelia Fort* by Rob Simbeck (Atlantic Monthly Press, New York, N.Y., 1999)

CHAPTER 4

Written sources:

Banner: Dec. 10, 1958; Dec. 17, 1958; Jan. 5, 1959; Jan. 7, 1959; Oct. 23, 1961; Oct. 24, 1961; Oct. 25, 1961; Nov. 2, 1961

Encyclopedia Americana (Grolier Inc., Danbury, Conn., 2000)

"McConnell to Cole to Berry," presentation by Robert C.H. Mathews, Jr., to the Coffee House Club, May 16, 1991

MNAA Slide Presentation Script – "Nashville International Airport: One of the Keys to Nashville's Future"

Nashville: The Faces of Two Centuries, 1780-1980, written and edited by John Egerton (Produced by Nashville! Magazine, Plus Media Inc., 1979)

Tennessean: Aug. 16, 1943; Feb. 20, 1944; May 9, 1957; July 15, 1957; July 16, 1957; Dec. 1, 1957; Dec. 2, 1957; Dec. 4, 1957; Dec. 8, 1958; Dec. 13, 1958; Dec. 15, 1958; Jan. 19, 1959

World Book Encyclopedia (World Book Inc., Chicago, Ill, 2001)

Web site:

www.faa.gov – "A Brief History of the Federal Aviation Administration and Its Predecessor Agencies;" "FAA Historical Chronology, 1926-1996"

CHAPTER 5

Interviews with:

Nelson Andrews, Edward F. "Eddie" Jones, Robert C.H. Mathews, Jr., Carolyn Tune, David K. "Pat" Wilson

Written sources:

Aviation in Tennessee by Jim Fulbright (Mid-South Publications, Goodlettsville, Tenn., C1998)

Banner: June 13, 1937

Colemere Handbook of City and County Government (Circa 1947)

"McConnell to Cole to Berry," presentation by Robert C.H. Mathews, Jr., to the Coffee House Club, May 16, 1991

MNAA Slide Presentation Script – "Nashville International Airport: One of the Keys to Nashville's Future"

Tennessean: Dec. 14, 1969; Feb. 4, 1970

Tennessee Code Annotated, Vol. 8 (Lexis Publishing, 2000)

Web sites:

www.faa.gov – "FAA Historical Chronology, 1926-1996"

www.mscaa.com – (Memphis Shelby County Airport Authority)

www.nashintl.com (Nashville International Airport)

www.tys.org (Knoxville Airport Authority)

CHAPTER 6
Interviews with:
Nelson Andrews, Edward F. "Eddie" Jones, Robert C.H. Mathews, Jr., Gen. William G. Moore, Jr., Carolyn Tune, David K. "Pat" Wilson

Written sources:
"McConnell to Cole to Berry," presentation by Robert C.H. Mathews, Jr., to the Coffee House Club, May 16, 1991
MNAA Slide Presentation Script – "Nashville International Airport: One of the Keys to Nashville's Future"
Banner: April 28, 1977
Tennessean: Jan. 11, 1976; April 29, 1977; May 1, 1977

Web sites:
www.atlanta-airport.com (Hartsville Atlanta International Airport)
www.faa.gov – "FAA Historical Chronology, 1926-1996"
www.nashintl.com (Nashville International Airport)

CHAPTER 7
Interviews with:
Richard Fulton, Robert Lamb "Bob" Hart, Robert C.H. Mathews, Jr., Gen. William G. Moore, Jr., David K. "Pat" Wilson

Written sources:
General William G. Moore, Jr.'s, biography
MNAA Slide Presentation Script – "Nashville International Airport: One of the Keys to Nashville's Future"

Web site:
www.nashintl.com (Nashville International Airport)

CHAPTER 8
Interviews with:
Robert C.H. Mathews, Jr., Gen. William G. Moore, Jr., Jack Vaughn, E.W. "Bud" Wendell

Written sources:
MNAA Slide Presentation Script – "Nashville International Airport: One of the Keys to Nashville's Future"
Tennessean: Aug. 30, 1987

Web site:
www.nashintl.com (Nashville International Airport)

CHAPTER 9
Interviews with:
Robert Lamb "Bob" Hart, Robert C.H. Mathews, Jr., Jack Vaughn, E.W. "Bud" Wendell

Written sources:
Inside Opryland USA Inc. company newsletter, Vol. 5, No. 8, October 1987
MNAA Slide Presentation Script – "Nashville International Airport: One of the Keys to Nashville's Future"
Tennessean: Aug. 30, 1987; Aug. 31, 1987; Nov. 10, 1989; Nov. 11, 1989

Web site:
www.nashintl.com (Nashville International Airport)

CHAPTER 10
Interviews with:
Nelson Andrews, Richard Fulton, Robert Lamb "Bob " Hart, Edward F. "Eddie" Jones, Robert C.H. Mathews, Jr., Gen. William G. Moore, Jr.

Written sources:

Fortunes, Fiddles & Fried Chicken – A Nashville Business History by Bill Carey (Hillsboro Press, Franklin, Tenn., 2000)

"McConnell to Cole to Berry," presentation by Robert C.H. Mathews, Jr., to the Coffee House Club, May 16, 1991

MNAA Slide Presentation Script – "Nashville International Airport: One of the Keys to Nashville's Future"

The Economic Role of Nashville International Airport (prepared by GKMG Consulting Services Inc., March 2001)

Tennessean: June 4, 2000 (Airport Extra special supplement)

Web sites:

www.faa.gov – "FAA Historical Chronology, 1926-1996"

www.nashintl.com (Nashville International Airport)

CHAPTER 11

Interviews with:

Nelson Andrews, Richard Fulton, Edward F. "Eddie" Jones, Gen. William G. Moore, Jr., Tom Seigenthaler, Jack Vaughn, E.W. "Bud" Wendell, David K. "Pat" Wilson

Written sources:

The Economic Role of Nashville International Airport (prepared by GKMG Consulting Services Inc., March 2001)

Fortunes, Fiddles & Fried Chicken – A Nashville Business History by Bill Carey (Hillsboro Press, Franklin, Tenn., 2000)

Tennessean: June 4, 2000 (Airport Extra special supplement); Aug. 20, 2001

Web site:

www.nashintl.com (Nashville International Airport)

CHAPTER 12

Interviews with:

Richard Fulton, Edward F. "Eddie" Jones, Robert C.H. Mathews, Jr., Gen. William G. Moore, Jr.

Written sources:

"McConnell to Cole to Berry," presentation by Robert C.H. Mathews, Jr., to the Coffee House Club, May 16, 1991

Nashville's 30-year Aviation Plan (completed and approved 1993)

Tennessean: April 26, 2001; June 8, 2001; July 2, 2001

Web site:

www.nashintl.com (Nashville International Airport)

CHAPTER 13

Interviews with:

Nelson Andrews, Richard Fulton, Robert Lamb "Bob" Hart, Edward F. "Eddie" Jones, Robert C.H. Mathews, Jr., Gen. William G. Moore, Jr., Carolyn Tune, Jack Vaughn, E.W. "Bud" Wendell, David K. "Pat" Wilson

Written source:

Banner: April 13, 1983

CHAPTER 14

Interviews with:

Nelson Andrews, Richard Fulton, Robert Lamb "Bob" Hart, Edward F. "Eddie" Jones, Robert C.H. Mathews, Jr., Gen. William G. Moore, Jr., Jack Vaughn, E.W. "Bud" Wendell, David K. "Pat" Wilson

Written sources:

Tennessee Code Annotated, Vol. 8 (Lexis Publishing, 2000)

General William G. Moore, Jr.'s biography
Web site:
www.nashintl.com (Nashville International Airport)

CHAPTER 15
Written sources:
Tennessean: April 8, 2001; Sept. 12, 2001; Sept. 13, 2001
"Is It Safe?" – report on *60 minutes II*, CBS Television Network, Fall 2001

APPENDIX C
Acknowledgements
The preparation of this book relied heavily on the institutional memory of many sources, and the writer and editors express special appreciation to many of them including:

General William G. Moore, Jr., a highly decorated career military pilot who rose from a World War II combat pilot to a four star general heading up the Military Airlift Command. Upon military retirement he served for 17 years as President of the MNAA;

Robert C.H. Mathews, Jr, chairman of the Mathews Co., a real estate development and construction firm, who served as a board member of MNAA for 22 years, 18 of those years as Chairman;

Nelson Andrews, chairman, Brookside Properties (a commercial properties development, management and investment firm); past chairman, Nashville Area Chamber of Commerce (1969-1970);

Richard Fulton, consultant, Fulton & Associates; former chairman of the board, Bank of Nashville; Mayor of Nashville (1975-1987); member, U.S. House of Representatives (1963-1975);

Robert Lamb "Bob" Hart, partner, Hart-Howerton in New York City; lead design architect for the Nashville International Airport Terminal;

Edward F. "Eddie" Jones, senior consultant, Dye, Van Mol & Lawrence; former executive vice president, Nashville Area Chamber of Commerce (1967-1987); retired editor, Nashville Banner (1987 to 1998);

Carolyn Tune, widow of John C. Tune, Jr., who was chief architect of the MNAA;

Jack Vaughn, chairman emeritus, Opryland Hospitality & Attractions Group, a division of Gaylord Entertainment Company; past member, Chamber of Commerce Aviation Committee;

E. W "Bud" Wendell, retired president & CEO, Gaylord Entertainment Company; past president, Nashville Area Chamber of Commerce (1975-77, 1982-84, 1989-91), past chairman (1990); and

David K. "Pat" Wilson, chairman, Cherokee Equity Corporation; member, MNAA Board of Commissioners (1970-1988).

CREDITS
Concept and first draft:
Seigenthaler Public Relations
Judy Mizell, Writer/Editor

Production and final editing:
Dye, Van Mol & Lawrence, Inc.
Edward F. Jones
Senior Consultant